The World of
Vermeer

LIFE WORLD LIBRARY

LIFE NATURE LIBRARY

TIME READING PROGRAM

THE LIFE HISTORY OF THE UNITED STATES

LIFE SCIENCE LIBRARY

GREAT AGES OF MAN

TIME-LIFE LIBRARY OF ART

TIME-LIFE LIBRARY OF AMERICA

FOODS OF THE WORLD

THIS FABULOUS CENTURY

LIFE LIBRARY OF PHOTOGRAPHY

THE TIME-LIFE ENCYCLOPEDIA OF GARDENING

THE AMERICAN WILDERNESS

THE EMERGENCE OF MAN

THE OLD WEST

THE ART OF SEWING

FAMILY LIBRARY:

   THE TIME-LIFE BOOK OF FAMILY FINANCE

   THE TIME-LIFE FAMILY LEGAL GUIDE

   THE TIME-LIFE BOOK OF THE FAMILY CAR

TIME-LIFE LIBRARY OF ART

The World of Vermeer

1632 - 1675

by Hans Koning
and
the Editors of TIME-LIFE BOOKS

Time-Life Books, Alexandria, Virginia

Time-Life Books Inc.
is a wholly owned subsidiary of
TIME INCORPORATED

FOUNDER: Henry R. Luce 1898-1967

Editor-in-Chief: Hedley Donovan
Chairman of the Board: Andrew Heiskell
President: James R. Shepley
Vice Chairman: Roy E. Larsen
Corporate Editor: Ralph Graves

TIME-LIFE BOOKS INC.
MANAGING EDITOR: Jerry Korn
Executive Editor: David Maness
Assistant Managing Editors: Dale Brown,
Martin Mann
Art Director: Sheldon Cotler
Chief of Research: Beatrice T. Dobie
Director of Photography: Melvin L. Scott
Senior Text Editor: William Frankel
Assistant Art Director: Arnold C. Holeywell

CHAIRMAN: Joan D. Manley
President: John D. McSweeney
Executive Vice President: Carl G. Jaeger
Executive Vice President: David J. Walsh
Vice President and Secretary: Paul R. Stewart
Treasurer and General Manager: John Steven Maxwell
Business Manager: Peter B. Barnes
Mail Order Sales Director: John L. Canova
Public Relations Director: Nicholas Benton

TIME-LIFE LIBRARY OF ART
SERIES EDITOR: Robert Morton
Associate Editor: Diana Hirsh
Editorial Staff for *The World of Vermeer:*
Text Editor: Harvey B. Loomis
Picture Editor: Kathleen Shortall
Designer: Paul Jensen
Assistant Designer: Leonard Wolfe
Chief Researcher: Martha T. Goolrick
Researchers: Harriet Delihas, Lynda Kefauver,
Susanna Seymour

EDITORIAL PRODUCTION
Production Editor: Douglas B. Graham
Assistant: Gennaro C. Esposito
Quality Director: Robert L. Young
Assistant: James J. Cox
Copy Staff: Rosalind Stubenberg (chief),
Muriel Clarke, Florence Keith
Picture Department: Dolores A. Littles,
Patricia Mave
Art Assistant: Nanci Earle

About the Author

Hans Koning (now the pen name of Dutch-born novelist Hans Koningsberger) has lived and worked in the United States since 1951. The author's lifelong interest in Vermeer, his keen appreciation of painting and his mastery of both Dutch and English have been especially advantageous in his research for this book. Mr. Koningsberger has published three novels, translated several art books and written scores of articles for American publications. His book *Love and Hate in China* is a comprehensive eyewitness report on Chinese life.

The Consulting Editor

H. W. Janson is Professor of Fine Arts at New York University, where he is also Chairman of the Department of Fine Arts at Washington Square College. Among his numerous publications are his *History of Art* and *The Sculpture of Donatello.*

The Consultant for This Book

Charles Seymour Jr., Professor of the History of Art at Yale University and Curator of Renaissance Art of the Yale University Art Gallery, has given invaluable assistance in the preparation of this volume. In 1964 Dr. Seymour published the pioneering article "Dark Chamber and Light-Filled Room: Vermeer and the Camera Obscura."

On the Slipcase

The head of Fame is shown in a detail from Vermeer's allegorical painting *An Artist in His Studio (page 164).*

End Papers

Front: This drawing of a boat slide is by Anthonie van Borssom.
Back: Amsterdam is seen from the north in this drawing by Lambert Doomer.

Editors' Note

Because Vermeer dated only two of his works and there is scholarly disagreement over an acceptable chronology, dates are not given with many illustrations of Vermeer paintings or with the works of other artists whose paintings cannot be dated with confidence. Since Vermeer left all his works unnamed, the editors have selected titles on the basis of scholarly agreement or the preference of owners.

The picture essays for this book were written by Dale Brown. The following individuals and departments of Time Inc. helped to produce the book: Editorial Production, Michael E. Keene Library, Benjamin Lightman; Picture Collection, Doris O'Neil; Photographic Laboratory, George Karas; TIME-LIFE News Service, Murray J. Gart; Correspondents Frisco Endt (Amsterdam), George Taber (Brussels), Maria Vincenza Aloisi (Paris), Elisabeth Kraemer (Bonn) and Barbara Moir (London).

Contents

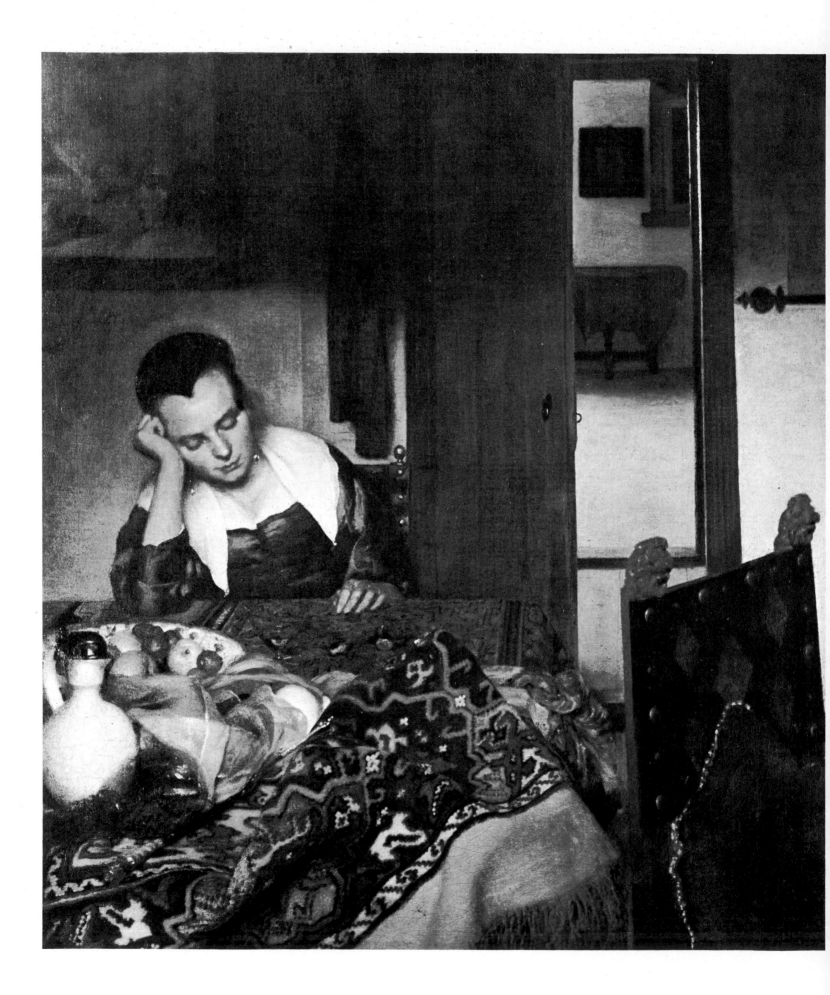

I

Art for a
Time of Reason

Of the great painters of the past three centuries, none has left so many unanswered questions about himself, his goals, theories and influences as the man who has been aptly called the "Sphinx of Delft." Few important artists have produced such a modest harvest of paintings for a lifetime of work and surely none has been virtually unknown for so long after his death. And yet few painters have left such a glowing legacy of genius as did Jan Vermeer. The calm, enigmatic expression of the *Girl Asleep* at left contains more clues to the artist who painted her than do the few recorded details of his life.

Vermeer was born in the town of Delft in 1632, near the zenith of an era that saw the Dutch nation lift itself into prominence as one of Europe's great powers. During this Golden Age, which spanned most of the 17th Century, Holland achieved unparalleled economic, social and political growth. In a brief period of about 75 years it produced a treasury of painting whose brilliance has rarely been surpassed.

Jan Vermeer was the last great master in the legion of artists who produced this explosion of art. By the time of his death at the age of 43 in 1675, the Golden Age was coming to an end; the nation and its art were in decline. Vermeer himself died apparently little known or esteemed and it was 200 years before his luminous, tranquil paintings were recognized as ranking among the great masterpieces of Western art.

Dutch 17th Century art was unique not only for its vast quantity and superb craftsmanship but also for the sharp realism with which it recorded the face of Holland and its people. Never before had a group of artists looked at the physical world around them with such clarity and set down their observations with such fidelity. Turning away from the religious, mythological and allegorical subjects that had been the themes of Renaissance art, they portrayed what they saw around them, with great artistry but without histrionics or affectation.

In 1632, the year Vermeer was born, another great Dutch painter, Rembrandt van Rijn, unveiled in Amsterdam an extraordinary painting that clearly expressed the new spirit. This painting was called *The Anatomy of Dr. Nicolaas Tulp,* and it showed five surgeons and doctors of

Taking subject matter as simple as this—a girl, a table, a room —Vermeer was able to construct a body of work which, though small, approaches true perfection. Not the least wonderful aspect of his art is its ability to attract people with its quietness and hold them fast with its sense of order.

Girl Asleep

medicine intently watching as a famous Dutch physician described the muscles and sinews in the dissected hand and forearm of a cadaver. (Two more figures were later added to the painting.)

Despite its frank subject matter and grimly realistic treatment, the painting was apparently regarded not with revulsion but rather with genuine interest. Indeed, the popular acclaim that the work received seemed to bespeak a general conviction among its beholders that the earth was a place of reason where one could study the awesome reality even of a dissected human body with equanimity. Rembrandt had faced his subject with unblinking directness, and he endowed it with dignity and beauty. Thus, he created a work of art filled with drama and a real sense of psychological focus—and his audience was ready for it.

It was not coincidence that this new emphasis on realism in art should have come when and where it did. The age that produced Rembrandt and Vermeer was one that saw the advent of reason as a guiding principle for the scientists and philosophers of Europe. One of the great spokesmen of the era, René Descartes, spelled out the Age of Reason's new faith in mathematical certainty and the power of rational philosophy in his *Discours de la méthode,* and the rationalist spirit of the day seems epitomized in his tenet, "I think, therefore I am."

Everywhere, men were moved to examine the reality of the physical world around them; they were in a fever to discover its laws. The musty traditions of Aristotelianism and Scholasticism were broken, mystery made way for experience, and observation supplanted superstition.

Astronomy came of age when Johannes Kepler coded the laws governing planets' behavior in 1609 and Galileo first observed the heavenly bodies through a telescope in 1610. In 1627 the English physician William Harvey explained his theory of the circulation of the blood, and 40 years later Robert Hooke made scientific history with the publication of *Micrographia,* a careful documentation of the microscopic world. In France Blaise Pascal made prodigious contributions to mathematics.

Throughout this time of intellectual ferment, Holland played a role of leadership far out of proportion to its size and visible resources. In fact it could fairly be said that the Age of Reason first flourished in the neat red-brick towns of the Dutch republic. It was no coincidence that Descartes, though a Frenchman, lived in Holland for 20 years and aired his epochal theories there, for, in Holland, religious tolerance, the prerequisite for the new rationalism, was written into law a century before other nations stopped burning their witches and heretics.

Science, too, was permitted to develop freely in Holland. The versatile physicist, astronomer and mathematician, Christian Huygens, developed the wave theory of light and also invented the pendulum clock. Leiden University built one of the first astronomical observatories. A scientific approach to the practice of medicine was pioneered by Dutch physicians. In the science of optics the Dutch were preeminent. The telescope that Galileo adapted for his researches had been invented by lens grinders of the Lowlands. The simple microscope was also first used in Holland, and a book of microscopic observations was printed in The Hague a decade before Hooke's *Micrographia* appeared. Many men—

including Descartes—were fascinated by the subject of light; Descartes wrote a treatise speculating—not very accurately—on what happened to the reality "seen" by the eye when it was interpreted by the mind.

The artists of Holland also were interested in the problem of seeing and in discovering new ways of treating visual reality. They strove to portray what they saw around them as naturalistically as possible. Many made careful studies of the laws of perspective; some were fascinated by the techniques of *trompe l'oeil* painting, which seeks to deceive the eye into seeing three dimensions in a flat surface. Some used newly discovered or improved optical devices that reduced the scenes they painted to images on ground glass or flat surfaces, in the belief that this provided the most exact image of reality.

Thus, the painters of 17th Century Holland, in their search for realism and their application of new techniques, reflected the rationalistic spirit of their age. But they also owed a strong debt to an earlier era of spiritual upheaval, the Reformation, which had precipitated a crisis in the function and position of the artist.

Until the 16th Century, artists customarily depended on long-established sources of patronage such as nobles, guild organizations and the Catholic Church. These individuals and institutions commissioned artists' work and provided a steady market for their output. The patrons also largely determined what the artists would paint. The subjects were, almost inevitably, Biblical themes rich in symbolism, allegorical and mythological scenes, or pictures that glorified the virtues of a wealthy patron.

But 17th Century Holland was dominated by neither Catholicism nor nobility. In a long and bitter war of independence, Holland had thrown off the Catholic rule of Spain and early in the 17th Century emerged as a Protestant, mercantile republic. Calvinism had taken strong hold in the new nation, and that stern creed had little use for religious art. Faced with the absence of traditional patronage, Dutch artists began working on their own and taking their chances in the market place.

This image of the free but insecure artist is a familiar one today, but then it was revolutionary. And while it gave the artist his freedom to paint what he liked and how he liked, it imposed very trying conditions on him. Art was very popular in Holland and the demand was great, but the supply was even greater. For the first time in the history of Western art there was a surplus of artists; the market became flooded and then depressed.

Furthermore, painters in those days functioned much like simple artisans and their paintings were, in fact, often sold from booths in the general market place, or in special buildings on market days. The competition was strenuous. Painters' guilds tried to regulate the traffic in art—no one could sell paintings except guild members—but in a buyers' market their control was not very effective. Art dealers sometimes agreed to take all of an artist's work, which gave him some security; but there were no exhibitions, as they are known today, in which a dealer might organize and show an artist's work for the public to buy. Some painters made profitable arrangements to sell their work outside the usual channels. One such bizarre contract was made between an artist and a sailor who owed him money. The artist painted a number of pictures, and the sailor paid off his debt by acting as agent, taking the pictures on his travels, selling them where he could and turning the profits over to the artist.

But for most artists in the Dutch Golden Age, earning a living by their art alone was a difficult, precarious business. Many were perpetually in debt; some turned to other trades and became, as well as artists, innkeepers, footmen, tax collectors, brewers. They also learned to specialize their artistic output. If an artist had luck selling a certain kind of painting, he adhered to that subject or style, often to the exclusion of all others. This imposed a limitation on the artists, and it made them even more dependent on the whims of the art buyer. But it also may have accounted in part for the great skill they achieved in their chosen fields.

Specialization also contributed to the separation of Dutch art into several distinct divisions. When the painters of Holland in effect traded the tyranny of the Church and court for that of a demanding public they quickly learned that what the public wanted to look at in painting was the likeness of their newly free country and its people. This interest seemed to develop naturally in four main categories: still life, portraiture, landscape and genre (the art of the everyday).

The first, still-life painting, was almost the invention of the Dutch Golden Age, and it has never been handled with more exquisite skill. It reflected the tastes of the new, bourgeois art patron and his interest in strictly representative art. But the everyday objects in still-life painting were often freighted with symbolic meanings, and they thus satisfied the Dutch moralistic temperament as well.

Portraiture developed within the new spirit of reason and reflected the Dutch people's pride in themselves and their achievements. In the work of Frans Hals and Rembrandt, portrait painting achieved a sensitivity and a realism that have never been surpassed.

Landscape art carried on a tradition that went back two centuries in Lowlands art. Early Flemish artists had portrayed their countryside extensively but always as background for Biblical or allegorical subjects. The new landscapists made the countryside itself their subject and learned to invest as much beauty and emotion in a picture of a lonely tree under a wide, storm-swept sky as their contemporaries in France and Italy put into a whole choir of angels.

Genre painting, too, had its roots in earlier Flemish art, particularly that of Pieter Brueghel, but it reached its zenith in the 17th Century. In the category of genre fall the many views of domestic interiors and taverns, milkmaids, drinkers and skaters, that are almost a trademark of Dutch art. Sometimes genre painting is anecdotal, sometimes simply reportorial, though it often conveys a subtle moral message. At its worst, genre is mere illustration; at its finest it is distinguished by superb technique, masterly composition and sharp psychological insight.

The events of history can be invoked to explain why the art of 17th Century Holland took these forms. But the question of why Dutch art was so good, why there were so many artists of genius at one time in one small nation, is a mystery no sociological investigation will ever be

The mysteries of sight excited the curiosity of 17th Century artists and scholars, including René Descartes, the great French philosopher who attempted to find a scientific explanation for the perception of reality. His diagram above, a mixture of fact and fancy, shows bulging eyes transmitting the image of an arrow to the brain's pineal gland, which Descartes believed housed man's soul.

likely to answer. Whatever the reason, at about the turn of the 17th Century, Holland suddenly started to produce an astonishing number of great artists. A list of the painters of the Golden Age—naming only undisputed masters—resembles the catalogues of a great museum:

Frans Hals, the first of the "modern" portraitists, was born about 1580. Five years later came Hendrick Avercamp and then, about 1590, Hercules Seghers; these two men stand at the beginning of Dutch landscape painting. (One is tempted to say that the Dutch invented landscape—the English word itself is probably derived from the Dutch word *landschap.*) They were followed by the landscape artist Jan van Goyen, born in 1596, and Simon de Vlieger, born in 1601, whose specialty was seascapes. Next came Rembrandt in 1606 and at about the same time Adriaen Brouwer, first of the great genre painters.

Then it was as if the sluice gates were opened. Adriaen van Ostade (1610) and Gerard Terborch (1617) were distinguished genre painters, and the latter was a fine portraitist as well. Also born in 1617 was Emanuel de Witte, whose specialty was church interior scenes that were masterpieces of perspective. Philips Koninck (1619) was a landscapist, Carel Fabritius (1622) a remarkable master of Amsterdam and Delft, who died early, leaving only a few pictures which seem to have had great impact on the young Vermeer. Willem Kalf (1622) was a still-life painter, Jan Steen (1626) was in the highest rank of genre painters. Jacob van Ruisdael (about 1630) became the greatest landscapist of all. Pieter de Hoogh and Gabriel Metsu (1629) were genre painters, De Hoogh the most popular of his day. Vermeer was born in 1632 and Nicolaes Maes, another genre artist, in 1634.

After that, the stream suddenly ran dry.

Over a period of 75 years these great men and hundreds of lesser painters turned out a veritable flood, literally hundreds of thousands, of paintings—not all masterpieces, but consistently at an astonishingly high level of craftsmanship. "There can surely be no other country in the world," wrote a 17th Century Frenchman who taught at the University of Leiden, "where there are so many, and such excellent, paintings."

Amid all this artistry, the painting of Rembrandt and Vermeer stands out as being the product of genius that rises above the idiom of time and place. Rembrandt was Dutch but universal. His genius ranged far beyond the categories and specialties that many Dutch painters worked in. His *Anatomy of Dr. Nicolaas Tulp,* which seems to sum up an entire age, was painted when he was only 26. A portraitist without peer, he took as subjects everyone from rich burghers to indigent peddlers and left at least 80 self-portraits; he was a landscapist and a painter of Biblical and allegorical scenes, all illuminated by a glowing, golden light that came to be his special signature. He was, in a sense, a world of art in himself.

It would be hard to imagine an artist more different from Rembrandt than Jan Vermeer. In the first place, whereas Rembrandt at one time enjoyed fame and wealth and had hundreds of commissions, Vermeer seems to have made comparatively little impression on his contemporaries; only three references to his stature as an artist have come down to us from his own day. From what evidence we have, it is clear that, unlike the flamboyant Rembrandt, who produced hundreds of paintings and thousands of drawings, Vermeer led a quiet life and his artistic production was small. Fewer than 40 works by Vermeer are known today; no one knows how many paintings—if any—he sold during his lifetime.

His subject matter was extraordinarily restricted. Almost all his paintings are apparently set in two smallish rooms in his house in Delft; they show the same furniture and decorations in various arrangements and they often portray the same people, mostly women. The women are seen doing simple, domestic tasks—working in the kitchen, making lace, playing a musical instrument, writing, primping. There is little that resembles many busy contemporary interiors; in fact, there is practically no movement at all. The French author Marcel Proust wrote about Vermeer's pictures, "They are all fragments of the same world: a world that is always—with whatever genius it is re-created—made up of the same table, the same rug, the same woman, the same fresh and unique beauty."

The *Girl Asleep (page 8)* is an early work of Vermeer, generally thought to have been painted when he was in his mid-twenties, but it shows many of the objects and structural devices that are familiar in his later work. The leather-backed, brass-studded chairs with two lion heads on top, the rich Persian rug, bunched in folds and used as a tablecloth, the white ceramic pitcher, the map on the wall to the right of the door, all appear in many later paintings. The unexpected, almost abrupt interposition of the chair and table in the foreground, which gives the effect of separating the subject from the viewer by a physical object as well as by distance, is an arrangement Vermeer used in at least a dozen paintings.

There are also a few respects in which the *Girl Asleep* differs from Vermeer's mature work. The colors of the earlier picture include some striking reds and browns, whereas the later work is dominated by delicate harmonies of blue and yellow. After *Girl Asleep,* Vermeer never again used the device of an open door leading to another room behind the subject—though it was an arrangement very popular with genre painters of the day.

At first glance, *Girl Asleep* would seem to have been made to order for the bustling Dutch market place of portraits, still lifes and genre scenes. Vermeer should have been able to paint his way to fame and riches by turning out pictures of cooks, kitchens and domestic interiors in any number of variations to adorn dozens of 17th Century living rooms.

But he didn't, and if we look more closely at his work, we begin to see why. Only at first glance is Vermeer's *Girl Asleep* similar to the *Sleeping Girl* by his contemporary Nicolaes Maes, or to the many other pictures of the same subject deftly painted by the other great genre painters. The other paintings tempt one to smile: here is a lazy servant girl who will be in trouble when her mistress returns; one feels a sensuality in the defenselessness of a girl asleep, watched but unaware. These evocations seem appropriate in a picture intended for the living room, and they do much to explain the enduring quality of Dutch genre painting.

But there is none of this warm, easy atmosphere about Vermeer's girl. One cannot guess who she is, why she sleeps, what she dreams. It has even been suggested that the girl is really lost in thought and not sleeping at all, but the painter has given no clue. There is nothing anecdotal here, nothing amusing. The girl is not posing. It is almost as if she were not so much a girl at a table as a pattern of color. She remains distant, cool, unfamiliar.

It would make a man uncomfortable to have such a painting overlooking the homey affairs of his living room, and this probably is why Vermeer did not fit the market place of his day. One imagines a prospective buyer muttering, "No, Vermeer is too cold and lifeless for my taste."

Today, we do not look at the rare Vermeers in our museums in the same frame of mind as a Dutch merchant shopping for a gift to his wife. For one thing, we have learned to see differently. Photography, by making it possible to preserve a moment of reality so it can be studied and absorbed, has trained the modern eye to be aware of things it might not be able to pick out for itself: how daylight coming in a window haloes a woman's head; how light glances off a gem or even off the crust of a loaf of bread; how much bigger a foreground object appears in relation to something in the background.

Vermeer saw these things with extraordinary clarity. Though his work is far from being photographic in the sense that it merely mirrors a scene, Vermeer saw and recorded better than any painter of his time the precise appearance of objects as they are defined by light and space.

Furthermore, Vermeer's work is extremely modern in its personal quality. It may be that Vermeer did not miss out in the market place of his day but that he shunned it. He alone, among all his clever or brilliant colleagues, seemed to paint for himself only. In this he was far ahead of his time, for only in the last century has art generally become personal, as artists have learned to paint for themselves instead of trying to please an audience or to adhere to an artistic tradition.

It is this modern quality of Vermeer that led Proust to say of him, "He is an enigma in an epoch in which nothing resembled nor explained him." And yet, in another sense Vermeer's painting was unmistakably a part of the new art of his age. René Huyghe, former curator of paintings in the Louvre Museum, wrote in apparent contradiction of Proust, "Vermeer is . . . one of the most perfect symbols of his time and his country."

Both these comments, different as they sound, were aimed at the same point: Vermeer, though dealing with subjects familiar to the people and reproduced by the artists of his time, nevertheless added to these commonplace objects a luster and significance purely his own that made the scenes seem, after all, extraordinarily different. In a sense, he triumphed over the realism of his time: he treated real subjects with the utmost fidelity and then infused them with a personal insight that gives them a special quality of their own.

"His universe is secret, impenetrable and dominated by his ego," wrote Huyghe. "His poetry is steeped in his own epoch, draws all its strength from it—but only in order to reach the summit where it is isolated from, and dominates, the forest below." It is this private view of his world, illuminated by an uncanny clarity of light and color, that distinguishes the Master of Delft.

The concept of the painter shivering in a garret, depicted here by Pieter de Bloot, was originated in 17th Century Holland. Earlier artists had lived on the commissions of churches and noble patrons, but with the rise of the middle class, artists had to compete for popularity. Some supplemented their incomes by selling fabrics, dealing in art or running taverns in which paintings were displayed. Vermeer did all three.

The Paradox of Reality

Vermeer has often been called the great realist—but is he? His works—unlike those of his contemporaries, who concerned themselves with the here and now, with the world of 17th Century Holland—actually go far beyond the boundaries of "realistic" painting. In doing so, they raise a question fundamental to an understanding and appreciation of art; just what can be considered "real" in art? For example, there is the sense of suspended motion and time that pervades Vermeer's *Young Woman with a Water Jug (opposite).* Everybody has experienced such a fragile moment of heightened awareness when suddenly "time stands still." Vermeer has captured it again and again. In the same vein is the deep calm and quiet, the even light, which fill his paintings. Did he encounter this peacefulness in his real life—he who lived and worked in a house that contained an inn, that stood on a noisy market square and that sheltered his 11 children?

"A work of art," an astute critic once said, "is a fragment of nature seen through a temperament." It is the artist's temperament—going far beyond the mere facility of his hands—that can elevate a picture to a work of art. This is the artist's reality—not just imitated life —but a seeing beneath the surface of things, and it is this reality that links the timeless art of Vermeer to that of such diverse painters as those represented by examples of their work on the following pages.

Glowing with the soft bloom of Vermeer's paints, the *Young Woman with a Water Jug* embodies a strange reality of its own. In the years since it left the artist's house, its numberless shades and modulations of purest ultramarine blue have gradually intensified.

Young Woman with a Water Jug

16

Hans Hofmann: *Night Spell*, 1965

Andrew Wyeth: *Christina's World*, 1948

Which of these two paintings is the more real, Andrew Wyeth's *Christina's World (above)* or Hans Hofmann's abstraction, *Night Spell (opposite)*? The Wyeth would seem to be the obvious answer: it is, after all, a recognizable image, painted with meticulous care. But as Wyeth himself has said, he did not paint the picture from life, nor did he have a story in mind. He had seen the crippled woman crawling in the field, and the sight of her, just that once, had been enough to stimulate his imagination. He went down into the field and made a quick sketch of the house before starting on the painting in his studio. That was all. "You see," he said, "my memory was more of a reality than the thing itself."

The late Hans Hofmann, by contrast, commenced with an ideal—the desire both to animate and to light up the empty white surface of his canvas with color. Art was to him "a created reality" and such a reality he has created here, without resort to representation of any kind. His painting, by setting out to be nothing more than itself—paint on canvas—is real; *Christina's World*, by Wyeth's own statement, is a painted memory.

To the 20th Century viewer, the *Annunciation Altarpiece* by Robert Campin looks real enough, providing as it does a glimpse of a bourgeois Flemish home of the 15th Century; but to the viewer of 500 years ago, it conveyed far more. Religion at that time was so powerful a force that God's spirit could be glimpsed under almost

Robert Campin: *Annunciation Altarpiece*, c. 1425

every aspect of the everyday world. Thus Campin could place the Virgin in this commonplace setting because the ordinary objects surrounding her actually stood for unreal and intangible things—recognizable symbols to such people as the donors of the altarpiece, seen kneeling in the left wing panel. The cloth under the Virgin's book, the lily,

the towel, the basin—all these symbolize the Virgin's purity. Even the mousetrap on Joseph's workbench in the right panel has a specific meaning: it symbolizes the Cross, for according to St. Augustine, the Cross, with Jesus as the bait, was the trap that caught the devil and in turn helped set mankind free for all time from the devil's grip.

21

Edvard Munch: *The Cry*, 1893

In marked contrast to Campin's altarpiece which looked real and was not, these two works by the modern Expressionists Paul Klee and Edvard Munch seem utterly unreal. Yet both artists clearly intended them to portray a very vivid reality, and they do: the reality of a primary emotion—namely, fear.

In *The Cry (above)*, Munch has projected fear with a visceral intensity; he has made something internal external, something intangible tangible. The anxiety that tears through the slender figure with the death's head emerges at the oval mouth as a scream which reverberates throughout the entire landscape, twisting and turning back upon itself in broad swaths of bilious-colored paint which suggest that there can be no relief from fear of this kind.

Klee, on the other hand, in his *Mask of Fear (opposite)*, has trained his eye inward. From his unconscious he has brought forth the multilegged creature opposite which totters along under its fearful burden, its eyes frozen into the unseeing stare of an oculist's signboard. Whereas Munch's figure projects its anxiety out on the world, Klee's parody of introverted man keeps its fear locked up inside it, behind a mask that is also a shield.

22

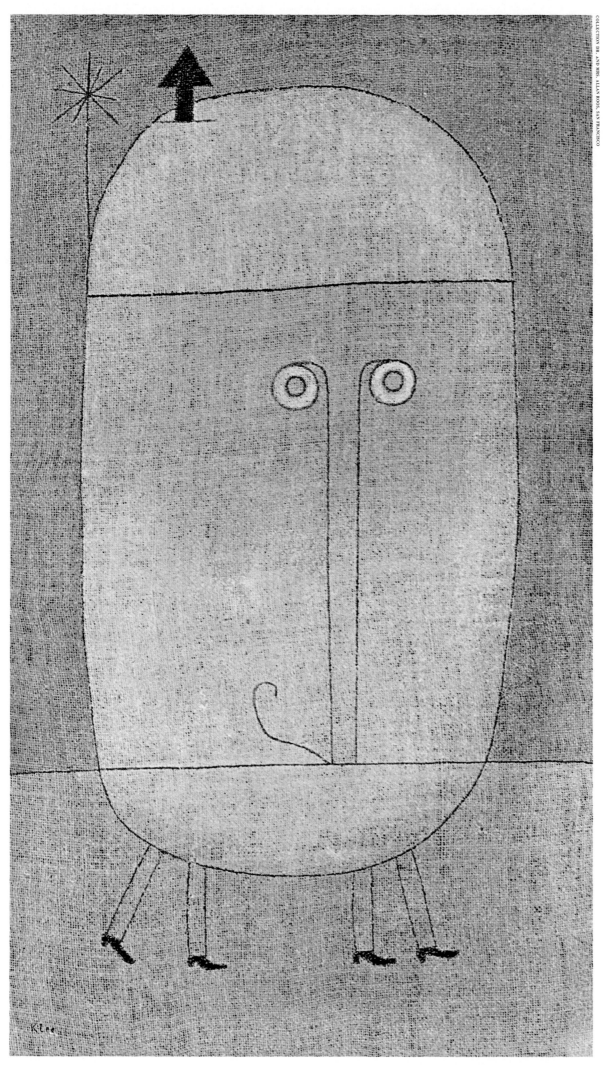

Paul Klee: *Mask of Fear*, 1932

Mark Tobey: *Broadway*, 1942   Mark Tobey: *Universal City*, 1951

For those artists who concern themselves with recording what they see, a challenging question might well be: is anything ever as it seems? Sitting all day long in front of two haystacks, the French Impressionist Claude Monet watched both change color with each change in light and made more than a dozen studies of them; two views painted at different hours are reproduced opposite. In thus portraying a single telling moment each time—rendering "my impressions in the face of the most fugitive effects"—Monet achieved freshness and spontaneity. He thus came closer than any artist before him to closing the gap between art and nature—to capturing perceptual reality.

By demonstrating that the thing observed can differ from one moment to the next, Monet raised another question: if nothing is ever exactly as it was, cannot a concept of something be more real than the thing itself? The American artist Mark Tobey is one painter who has tried to answer this question in his paintings of what might be called conceptual reality. It is Tobey's *concept* of a city that is the subject of the works above. The first, *Broadway,* was done not in New York, but in Devonshire, England, where it was so dark and quiet at night that "you could hear the horses breathing." Yet Tobey was able—at this great remove—to fill his canvas with the lights, the charged excitement and somehow even the noise of Broadway. In the second painting, Tobey has dissolved the vestiges of imagery and perspective of the first version into an amalgam of crowded, jostling brush strokes which without showing anything familiar nevertheless suggest powerfully the dynamism and pressures of the great metropolis.

Claude Monet: *Two Haystacks*, 1891

Claude Monet: *Two Haystacks*, 1891

The one reality all artists have in common is light, which makes visible everything they paint. Without it, there would be no art, and many are the artists who have been drawn to light as the very source of their being, making light itself the subject of their paintings. Monet is of course a prime example; Vermeer to an important degree is another. Even Hans Hofmann, in the nonobjective work seen earlier, can be said to have painted light, since his flashing colors are nothing more than what the poet Goethe called "the deeds of light."

Vermeer's fascination with light manifested itself in many ways, but especially in the still life, for here was an opportunity to transform and ennoble simple arrangements of simple things, like the basin and pitcher in the detail opposite from *Young Woman with a Water Jug (page 17)*. The 18th Century French painter Chardin *(below)* shared this fascination, one reason why he is often compared to Vermeer. And in the examples of their works shown here, both men reveal a touch so subtle that it borders on the magical: while giving shape to things, the light also seems to be dissolving them in reflections of itself. Cup your hands over Vermeer's pitcher so that they conceal its form, and it becomes unrecognizable. All that is left is paint—paint that creates a light of its own.

Jean-Baptiste Siméon Chardin: *The Silver Goblet*, c. 1759

28

II

The Golden Age

On the evening of June 5, 1648, fireworks and bonfires in all the towns of the United Provinces celebrated victory for the Dutch in their war of independence. That morning at 10 o'clock sharp the terms of the peace treaty with Spain had been read out in a sober ceremony in the Dutch Supreme Court of Justice in The Hague.

The ceremony was planned with a dramatic sense of timing. On another June 5 at 10 o'clock in the morning precisely 80 years earlier, the war had begun, to all intents and purposes, with the execution of two of Holland's first revolutionaries. They were the Counts of Egmont and Hoorn, who had sought some relief for their country from the oppressive rule of the King of Spain. Instead of negotiating with them, the King's representative in the Netherlands had taken them prisoner. Then, before a mute crowd in Brussels, they were beheaded, and the people pushed past the Spanish soldiers to dip their handkerchiefs in the blood of the first martyrs of the long war.

The story of that bitter conflict has a place in any account of Jan Vermeer's career. It was still going on when Vermeer was born (as it had been when his father—and probably his grandfather—were born); more important, it shaped the character of the whole Dutch nation, and had a direct effect on the development of 17th Century Dutch art.

Jan Vermeer and his fellow artists worked in an age when almost every facet of men's lives underwent drastic changes wrought by the war and the violent events accompanying it. Holland emerged from these upheavals as an aggressive, Protestant republic with a capitalistic economy and a bourgeois society. These cultural conditions produced a climate in which artists suddenly flourished like flowers in a hothouse. It was almost as if the war had brought together all the ingredients necessary for the spontaneous generation of an artistic flame.

The rebellion that flared after the Counts of Egmont and Hoorn were executed in 1568 had actually started brewing more than a decade earlier. At that time Charles V, the Holy Roman Emperor, abdicated; he left Spain and the 17 provinces of the Low Countries to his son, Philip II. The people of the Lowlands were accustomed enough to outside

Prince William of Orange, the defender of Dutch liberty, projects the cool nerve of a man who could—and did—stand up to the Spanish King in Holland's struggle for self-determination. Outlawed by the enraged monarch, he was later assassinated.

Michiel Jansz. van Miereveld: *Prince William of Orange*, 1620

29

rule—their land had been subjected to foreign intervention since the Middle Ages. They had had no quarrel with Charles V, who in the first place was one of them, having been born in Ghent, and who had allowed them a high degree of autonomy in conducting their own affairs.

But Philip was a different sort of man. Morose, dictatorial, fanatically Catholic, the new King hated the north, and cared for nothing but Spain and his religion. In August 1559, he paid a brief visit to the Lowlands and coldly addressed the territory's notables, the members of the parliamentary States-General. He demanded of the Dutch a three-million-guilder tribute to Spain in addition to the taxes already being paid, suppression of all Protestant sects and submission to his half-sister Margaret, the Duchess of Parma, whom he had made regent of the Lowlands. Philip then bade a hostile farewell to the States-General and set sail for Spain, which he never left again.

The first effect of Philip's harsh policies, enforced by the Duchess of Parma, was to arouse the Lowlands' Protestants, already inflamed by the anti-Papist preaching of the Calvinists. A wave of religious rebellion swept the country. Crowds attacked Catholic churches with Reformation zeal, threw down statues, and burned and smashed everything connected with the hated priesthood. One English observer said of such a riot that it "looked like hell where were above 1,000 torches brannyng and syche a noise! as yf heven and erth had gone together, with fallyng of images and fallyng down of costly works." Before the month-long holocaust was over, vast treasures of medieval art had been destroyed.

The Spanish answer was brutal and ruthless. In 1567, Philip sent the Duke of Alva and 10,000 troops north to replace the Duchess of Parma, and the years of the "Spanish Fury" followed. Town after town in the Lowlands was besieged, taken and ravaged. Alva executed his mission with a zeal that made him, and by extension all Spaniards, hateful to every Dutchman. He established a court called the "Council of Troubles" to try Netherlanders for heresy and sedition (Dutchmen called it the "Council of Blood"), and it was this court of injustice that sent the Counts of Egmont and Hoorn to their deaths. By 1568 groups of 30, 40 and 50 people at a time were being condemned to die; their property was confiscated by the Crown.

At this point the young nobility of the Lowlands began to take up arms against the oppressor. Later, the resistance to Spain became a democratic—or rather, a bourgeois—revolution; at first, however, it was led by princes and counts. The martyrs Egmont and Hoorn were among these, but the most prominent was Prince William of Orange *(page 28)*.

William's role is comparable to that played by George Washington 200 years later in the American Colonies: he was by every measure the father of the new republic. He quickly became the center of resistance in the fight, its voice, its general; he found the money and the troops. William was only 26 when King Philip left for Spain, but was already widely known as a brilliant diplomat and a man of culture as well as a dashing ladies' man. He was heir to the rich possessions of the family of Nassau in Germany, and he was also ruler of the tiny independent princedom of Orange in the south of France.

When Philip took over the Spanish crown, William was *Stadhouder* —the viceroy, or representative—of the King in the powerful Lowland provinces of Holland, Zeeland, Utrecht and Burgundy; at the outset, William and his followers took great pains to protest their continued loyalty to their overlord. Their fight, they stated repeatedly, was not against the Crown but against the tyranny and injustices perpetrated by the representatives of that Crown. (The Dutch national anthem stems from those days, and still contains a line in which William says, "I have always honored the King of Spain.") However, Alva's harshness and the King's refusal to compromise slowly pushed William toward an ever-more-extreme position. One is again reminded of the course of events leading to the American Revolution.

The first turning point in the war came in 1574, when the Spanish siege of Leiden was broken by Dutch seagoing guerrilla fighters called Sea Beggars. These were rough and ready mariners who banded into a semimilitary organization to bedevil the Spaniards wherever they could. Often they were more pirates than guerrillas, harassing peaceful shipping for their own benefit, and even occasionally raiding English coastal towns. William disapproved of their unsavory tactics and only reluctantly recognized them as part of his forces. They were, nevertheless, an effective weapon in the fight against Spain.

That the Sea Beggars were able to sail up to Leiden to lift the siege is a dramatic indication of the spirit in which the Dutch fought their rebellion. Leiden is not a port. Normally it is several miles from the sea. But in their dogged defense against the troops of the Duke of Alva, the people of Leiden had opened the dikes and flooded their land to hinder the foe; the Sea Beggars actually sailed in over the fields when they went to Leiden's rescue. Thousands of acres of farm land were spoiled by the flooding, but time and again during the war the Dutch made similar sacrifices—such as burning their own crops—to aid the fight against the hated Spaniard.

Five years after the successful defense of Leiden, eight of the northern provinces—Utrecht, Holland, Zeeland, Guelderland, Overijssel, Friesland, Groningen and Drenthe—signed a treaty called the Union of Utrecht. At the beginning of the war, each Dutch province had fought on its own under the loose control of William of Orange. Now these eight provinces were bound in a "firm union" for the common defense. Two years later they took the final step of rebellion: they abjured the King of Spain as their legal lord. The States-General met in 1581 to draw up a document in justification of their moral right to act:

"As it is apparent to all that a prince is constituted by God to be ruler of the people, and whereas God did not create the people slaves to their prince, to obey his commands, whether right or wrong, but rather the prince for the sake of the subjects . . . [then] when he does not behave thus, but, on the contrary, oppresses them . . . they may not only disallow his authority, but legally proceed to the choice of another prince for their defense."

The other prince they were turning to was William of Orange, and to King Philip it now seemed that this man was the sole cause of his troubles. Making the mistake of many statesmen before and since, Philip imagined that the war was kept going by a few men rather than by deep-seated social conflicts. So he issued an infamous "ban" which described William as "chief disturber of all Christendom and especially these Netherlands." To any man who would murder William, the ban offered forgiveness for all crimes, a patent of nobility from the Spanish crown, and 25,000 gold crowns.

Prince William's court was in Delft, which, being strategically located and easily defendable, was a stronghold of the revolutionary cause. (At this time there was no hint of the fame Delft would earn as an art center 50 years later.) There, on July 10, 1584, while William was meeting with the States-General to establish a national government, a fanatic Catholic named Balthasar Gérard sneaked into the Prince's house and shot him dead. Gérard, who had spent two years on his plot, was immediately captured, and his only reward was a quick trial, torture and death at the hands of an outraged citizenry.

In the confusion that followed its leader's death, the cause of Dutch freedom did in fact suffer for a while, but Holland's anger over its hero's death was too intense to burn out. William's son Maurice took over as commander-in-chief and the fighting went on. More towns were captured and recaptured; soldiers killed and were killed; peasants saw their houses and harvests burned time and again. One region of the southern Netherlands changed hands 25 times in 11 years.

Actually, though the men of the time could not perceive it, the war had already been decided at the time of William's death. No assassination, no siege, no battle could undo the inexorable shift of the war in favor of Holland. For the Dutch revolution was, of course, not the brainchild of one man or his family. The Renaissance and the Reformation had swept aside the circumstances in which nations and populations could be passed around and inherited like so much real estate. There was no longer any bond strong enough to keep the people of Amsterdam in one empire with the monarch in Madrid.

At last, in 1600, the trend of battle became clear when the Dutch won a decisive victory at the Battle of Nieuwpoort *(pages 44-45)*. Though final peace would not be achieved for almost 40 years, a temporary truce was signed in 1609, and Holland was never again threatened by the Spanish armies. For all practical purposes, the United Provinces were free to develop as an independent nation from the first years of the century.

Those years also ushered in the Golden Age of art, with the first paintings from the easels of Frans Hals, Hercules Seghers and Hendrick Avercamp. In fact, so closely did the birth of the new school of painting coincide with the birth of the nation that a French art historian has remarked that it was as if "the right of having a free and national school of painting" had been "part of the stipulations of the treaty of 1609."

This new school of painting was actually a branch of the Flemish art that in earlier centuries had produced such masters as the Van Eycks, Hieronymus Bosch and Pieter Brueghel. But while Flemish masters such as Rubens and Van Dyke continued brilliantly into the 17th Century in the traditional vein of European art, the Dutch school moved on its own way toward an ever-more-searching realism, and established itself as a separate stream.

The evolution of these two schools of painting was clearly related to the political developments of the day. When the eight northern provinces formed their "firm union," they created a permanent division within the Lowlands, drawing a boundary that has stayed much the same to the present day. The southern provinces that did not join the union— comprising modern Belgium—were neither able nor particularly anxious to break their bonds with Catholic Spain. The social system in the south was still feudal, dominated by an aristocracy that was largely French-speaking and not nationally oriented. What Protestants there were in the south fled north; many of these were businessmen from Antwerp, and their loss debilitated the southern provinces as much as did the continued Spanish occupation there. It would be two centuries before Belgium emerged as a stable, independent nation.

The northern region—which came to be known as Holland after its biggest, most prosperous province—flourished. The war had not only set the boundaries of the new nation (as an 18th Century chronicler put it, "Mars had stood over the birth as midwife") but it had also changed its spirit. Most of the old liberal men of noble birth had died during the war; the new leaders were merchants and Protestants. The aggressiveness, the national pride and hatred of Spain that had been stirred up by the war were now employed in developing the strong, mercantile economy that such a small nation needed to survive among its large neighbors. With almost a crusading spirit the Dutch began pushing Holland to greatness—and their weapon was trade.

Trading was nothing new for Holland. In the 14th Century, Dutch ships had begun carrying grain and timber from the Baltic Sea ports to Western Europe and the Iberian Peninsula. On the return trip north they carried spices and other valuable goods brought from the East Indies by Portuguese ships. But then Philip II closed down all Portuguese and Spanish ports to Dutch ships, and the merchants of Holland were forced to sail to the East themselves and trade there directly. In 1597 the first three Dutch ships to make the round-trip voyage returned to Amsterdam; of the crew of 249 men only 89 had survived. Nevertheless, the following year 22 more ships left for the Far East, and from then on the number increased steadily and rapidly. In 1600, the first Dutch ship reached Japan, and presently the Dutch were the only Europeans allowed to trade there. In 1601, Oliver van Noort, former pirate and Rotterdam innkeeper, sailed west through the Strait of Magellan to the Moluccas, south of the Philippines, and home around Africa; he was only the fourth captain in history to sail around the world (after one Portuguese and two Englishmen).

It was always trade, rather than colonizing, that provided the prime motivation for Dutch expansion, yet a colonial empire emerged in the process. The mariners built strong points on distant shores to protect their ships and stores from natives or marauding European ships; the strong points became forts, the forts led to further conquests. In 1605 the Dutch drove the Portuguese from the Moluccas; in 1618 they established a settlement called Batavia on Java *(page 47)*; in 1624 they founded New Amsterdam in America; by 1630 they controlled trading on the northeast coast of Brazil and by 1660 had taken over from the Portuguese on Ceylon.

In European waters, by the middle of the 17th Century, the Dutch merchants were handling three quarters of the enormous Baltic grain trade and they virtually monopolized the Bordeaux wine trade. Even Spain relied so heavily on the cargoes carried by Dutch ships that the embargo on them in Spanish ports was relaxed. Dutch vessels had become the freight carriers of Europe.

It was an enormously profitable situation for the merchants of Amsterdam and the other investors in Holland and Zeeland. Some of these shrewd businessmen had agricultural holdings, particularly in the western provinces; but the big financial returns were to be realized in maritime trade. Even the smallest merchant bought himself a share in some shipping venture or another.

The highest rewards came from the trade in spices, the most coveted product of the East Indies. Spices such as black pepper, cloves and cinnamon helped preserve and make palatable the dreary food of an age whose only other means of food preservation were pickling and salting. The lure of spices became as strong as the lure of gold; in the greedy struggle for East Indian resources in such places as Batavia and Ceylon, Dutch, Spanish, Portuguese and eventually English traders killed one another and any of the local population who stood in their way. Rather than see prices go down or leave something for a competitor, they burned down plantations, deported entire villages and turned the natives into virtual slaves.

All this was strictly a business operation. For example, in 1644 the Board of the Dutch East India Company stated that their holdings in the Far East were not Dutch conquests but "the property of private merchants, who were entitled to sell those places to whomever they pleased, even if it were to the King of Spain." These policies paid enormous dividends to the investors in the trade. One venture in 1599 made a 400 per cent profit, and from 1630 on, annual dividends of 30 per cent and more became normal for investors in the East India Company. (On the other side of the globe, in the West Indies, Dutch seamen also sometimes found ready-made profits: after Admiral Piet Hein's capture of a $50 million Spanish silver fleet in 1628, the West India Company paid a 75 per cent dividend.)

Later in the 17th Century, tea became a popular item in the tropical trade. The same Doctor Tulp whom Rembrandt had immortalized in his *Anatomy of Dr. Nicolaas Tulp* started a great fad for tea by prescribing it for all ills; he is said to have made his patients drink 50 cups of tea a day. A colleague wrote a little book, subsidized by the East India Company, extolling tea's virtues—perhaps the first-known example of the "Doctors recommend. . . ." technique of advertising.

Another popular Far Eastern product was porcelain. In the first half of the 17th Century, the Dutch imported and shipped on to the rest of Europe more than three million pieces of Chinese porcelain. The interest in porcelain led to the creation of the famous Delft Blue pottery industry, which still thrives. By 1700 Delft Blue pottery makers had become so proficient that they were exporting pieces of mixed Oriental and Dutch design back to Japan.

By no means all the goods brought in from abroad were sent on to foreign markets. Many of them stayed in Holland, as contemporary

Stimulated by the influx of bankers and merchants fleeing from the Spanish-held Southern Netherlands, Amsterdam by 1620 had become the busiest commercial center and seaport in Northern Europe. This contemporary etching—an allegory by Claes Jansz. Visscher—shows the Virgin of Amsterdam seated amidst symbolic riches brought to the banks of the River IJ: camels, elephants and monkeys represent India and Arabia; jewels and porcelain stand for China, and Indians recall the Americas. On the right, Dutch fishermen display Holland's most valuable export, and afloat in the river are ships of the Dutch East India Company.

paintings clearly testify. Tobacco was as popular then as now—it was first brought from the West Indies and the Americas in the 1500s—and the unsavory dens where the common man enjoyed his smoke made a favorite subject for such genre painters as Adriaen Brouwer and Adriaen van Ostade. Other products, faithfully recorded in the art of the day, added a cosmopolitan touch of luxury to the homes of the merchants who had gambled fortunes to import them: besides porcelain there were fine silk and satin fabrics, rare woods, and Turkish carpets (used as rugs, wall hangings or tablecloths). All of these appeared as props in hundreds of paintings of interior scenes, particularly those of Jan Vermeer.

Most of these goods had come into Holland through the port of Amsterdam, whose importance as a commercial center grew prodigiously. Its Commercial Exchange, established in 1585 after the Spanish captured the trading center of Antwerp, prospered enormously and occupied one of the most splendid buildings in the city. Amsterdam's Bank of Exchange, founded in 1609, set up a credit system, a stable rate of exchange and an efficient arrangement of checking accounts. By 1650 Amsterdam had become the focal point not only of Holland's trade network, but also of the European Money market.

Many elements contributed to Holland's sudden upsurge. In addition to the fervor inspired by the challenge of war, there was the effect of the new religion; many historians have suggested a strong correlation between the advent of Protestantism and the rise of capitalism. Although the great merchants of Holland were not the most ardent Calvinists ("They prefer gain to Godliness," complained the staunch English Protestant, Oliver Cromwell), their new religion, by glorifying hard work, thrift and sobriety, and by emphasizing the value of labor and the common man, provided the right psychological climate for a capitalistic economy. Another vital factor in Holland's remarkable growth was its position on the very edge of the continent, where it served as a natural gateway to Europe.

Lastly, Holland's wealth was created partly by the default of its neighbors. These countries were amazed and annoyed by Holland's success and consoled themselves by thinking it could not last long. The truth was that these nations, land wealthy but economically backward, were still bound by the fetters of feudalism and ancient financial practices. The Dutch not only initiated new, efficient trading methods, but they also understood sooner than most some of the laws of modern capitalism involving credit, interest and investment.

The men who profited most from this knowledge, and who became the key figures in all aspects of Dutch society, were the merchants of the nation's great cities—Amsterdam, The Hague, Utrecht, Delft and Haarlem. Not only were they financial leaders, but they also controlled the powerful town councils that served as local governments and directed the provincial States-General that met in The Hague to haggle over national policy. Since the Middle Ages, the town councils had been made up of the "most wise and rich" citizens: now, with trade the lifeblood of the country, the "most wise and rich" simply meant the most successful merchants. Thus during the entire 17th Century, the Netherlands was governed by a mercantile upper middle class, a business oligarchy of some 10,000 families.

Just as surely as they guided Holland's politics and economics, these prosperous merchants were also instrumental in the development of Dutch art. The average burgher was newly rich and perhaps more inclined to business than to esthetics, but he was probably aware of the Lowlands' old artistic traditions. He had plain tastes, but was fond of material things, and had the money to indulge his pleasure. Paintings were an ideal investment: not only were they decorative (and undoubtedly helpful to his image as a man of substance); they were also portable and to some extent negotiable, an important consideration to a man of speculative interests and fluctuating income.

As a firm Protestant, the average burgher had no interest in traditional ornate religious art. Even his churches were stark and whitewashed, with only the organ for artistic embellishment. As a sturdy bourgeois he wanted no part of the elaborate architecture and decor favored by the nobility of other countries. What he did want was a familiar landscape, a simple scene of everyday life or, best of all, a portrait of himself in his new dignity as a free citizen, with his family, his colleagues, or doing good works for some charitable group. He was proud of his house and of his way of life, and it made perfect sense to decorate the one with pictures of the other.

The artists, now completely reliant on the private citizen's patronage, responded to his demands with an energy and genius that more than matched the vigor and imagination of the merchants themselves. The result was not only a vivid portrait of a nation and a time but a brilliant chapter in art history as well.

From the pictorial record left by this artistic outburst, as well as from accounts of contemporary writers, a clear image emerges of what life was like for the country's middle classes amidst all the fighting, trading and speculating. After 1600, there was very little left of the aristocratic way of life in the United Provinces. The new republican society had shorn itself of its worldly and ecclesiastic princes. The House of Orange maintained a small court at The Hague which boasted a coterie of elegant, French-speaking, dueling gallants; but the general tenor of life was set by the merchants. There were few visible class distinctions among these men, and their houses reflected their simple tastes. Ostentation went against the grain—because they were Protestants, because they had just emerged from the austerity of the war and because their business ventures by their very nature were highly speculative—and a man's house, like the things in it, was an investment that he might have to dispose of at any moment.

So the furniture of a middle-class house at the beginning of the century was not very different from what would have been found in the late Middle Ages: a few tables, cupboards, a linen closet, several alcove beds built into the walls, a desk. The mantelpiece might be decorated, and the walls of the best room might have wainscoting, but the rest of the rooms were whitewashed.

Above all, the house was clean. Contemporary travelers from England,

France and Italy, after noting the abundance of food and absence of beggars in Holland, often exclaimed about the immaculate appearance of the interiors. One Frenchman wrote: "Dutchwomen pride themselves on the cleanliness of their house and furniture to an unbelievable degree. They never seem to stop washing and scrubbing all the wooden furniture and fittings." Another visitor added, "They would prefer to die of hunger surrounded by their shining cauldrons and sparkling crockery rather than prepare any dish that might possibly disarrange this perfect symmetry"—an observation that seems not quite so far-fetched after a study of the spotless kitchens portrayed in so many 17th Century canvases.

Later, as Holland prospered, some domestic luxuries began to appear as evidence of accumulated wealth—a change recorded in the paintings of the last half of the century. Gradually the decoration became more refined as walls were covered with tapestry or gilded leather. Now came the satins, rugs and porcelains; oak gave way to fine Oriental woods; tea tables, mosaics, marble, bronze and crystal artifacts were imported to grace the more elaborate houses.

Even with this new interest in luxuries, daily life for the most part remained simple. Beer was the main beverage for the well-to-do merchant's family, and his house had far fewer servants' rooms than a comparable establishment in France or England; the richest might employ one valet plus two maids for heavy household work. In all countries the middle classes were strong believers in simple virtues, in the family and the home, but there was an important difference in Holland: there the middle class set the tone for the whole country.

One thing besides money and art that particularly concerned the Hollander was education. As early as the 16th Century, Erasmus had commented on the unusually high number of educated people in Holland, and in the mid-1600s the Portuguese emissary in The Hague reported with considerable exaggeration that "there is not a cobbler here who does not add French and Latin to his own language." By the middle of the 17th Century, the Netherlands could boast five universities with such fine international reputations that more than half their students came from abroad.

The high level of literacy led to a flourishing printing trade in Dutch-language books. Most popular was the Bible, in a new official Dutch translation; next came the poems of Jacob Cats, whose homilies and morality verses were found in almost every town household—by 1665 an illustrated collection of Cats's works had sold 50,000 copies. Books about the new voyages and adventures in far countries were also sold in astounding numbers. The lack of censorship, moreover, made Holland, and especially Leiden, the clearing house for many works by refugees from England, France and Spain.

In 1584, cartographer Lucas Wagenaer published his *Mariner's Mirror,* two volumes of sailing directions and charts that were immediately translated, copied and pirated all over Europe. (In the English language such books are still called "Waggoners" by old-fashioned skippers.) From then until almost 100 years later, with the death of Johan Blaeu, son of the cartographer and map publisher Willem Blaeu, Dutch map making was the finest in Europe. For citizens ashore, it became fashionable to hang beautifully illustrated navigational charts on the walls of their houses as decoration—a fashion that is reflected in many contemporary paintings, as in Vermeer's *Officer and Laughing Girl (page 136)*.

Faithful as 17th Century Dutch art was in mirroring its age, there were a few aspects of contemporary life that were largely ignored by the painters. One was poverty. The prosperity enjoyed by Holland's middle classes did not extend to everyone. Much less wealth seeped down to the lowest classes than is often assumed from the neat streets and well-ordered households that appear in so many of the era's paintings. The workhouse, the poorhouse, slum living and child labor were all evident. A laborer worked 14 hours or more a day for a few pennies; an able seaman, who ran a 50-50 chance of not coming back from an Indies voyage, made two or three guilders a week, the equivalent of a weekly salary of about $10 today. Even though the Netherlands' standard of living compared favorably with that of any neighboring country, recent research shows that the Golden Age was far from golden for perhaps half the population.

The painters also ignored what had been the most important influence on their young nation: the war. Holland had spent decades fighting a bloody struggle, and yet there is practically no record of it in paintings except for a few sea battles and siege scenes. Soldiers there are in plenty, but they are shown enjoying themselves, and it is as if Hollanders had seen all the fighting and violence they could stand, and wanted no more of it in their art.

Furthermore, even when there was no fighting going on, the 17th Century was a time of rapidly changing fortunes and turbulent political crises—and yet little of this turmoil appears in the art. Most of the paintings cast an aura of calm well-being, an illusion that may well have represented the Dutchman's longing for a security and tranquillity he had never actually known. Though they look so solid in their pictures, the successful Dutch burghers must at times have had anxious moments when they wondered how they had come such a long way in so short a time, and whether it could last.

As a matter of fact, it did not. Eventually the prosperity of Holland became self-defeating: its covetous neighbors were finally moved to use force to acquire some of it for themselves. Toward the end of the age, the English wrested control of the seas from the Dutch Navy and in 1672 French troops overran most of the northern provinces. In a new era of surging nationalism, Holland was too small to maintain its dominant position. The merchants lost their daring; prosperity induced lethargy; godliness became self-righteousness. A long period of stagnation followed for Holland, and its art languished along with it.

But during most of the 17th Century, these tendencies had not yet come to the surface. That was the age that belonged to the men who had fought for and won their freedom: hard men, sober but given to sudden gambles; religious, proud and vain—the men who look at us from the portraits for which they posed with such obvious pride.

From War to Wealth

The serenity of Vermeer's art seems all the more remarkable when it is viewed against the turbulent background of his age. At that time, Holland was in the grip of a ruinous financial speculation over, of all things, the tulip—despite the fact that the Eighty Years' War was still going on. Before his own short lifetime ended, he would see his town shattered by a tragic explosion, his business as an art dealer wrecked by economic depression, and his country involved in two new wars. But even his paintings seem to say that his tranquillity was a narrow thing, its boundaries the rooms in which he worked. And his peace seems to have been gained not through quiet contemplation but by intense concentration. Vermeer worked just as hard to probe the visible world and its principal constituent—light—as did his fellow townsman, the pioneering microscopist Anton van Leeuwenhoek, to explore what until then had been an invisible world.

When the Dutch ripped off the chains of their Spanish oppressors, they seem also to have torn off their blinders. If there is a way to characterize the years of Vermeer's lifetime, it is perhaps as an age of observation. The eye was its central organ, as a student of the period has said, the lens its central instrument, and the anatomy of the universe its central pursuit. An age of observation, it was also an age of mass-visualization, and the Dutch were the greatest of its chroniclers.

Driven into the dunes by the tide, the Dutch and Spanish armies clash in a confusion of men, armor and horses, while ships of the opposing navies fire upon each other at sea. Fought and won by the Dutch on July 2, 1600, the Battle of Nieuwpoort ushered in the golden years of Holland's culture.

Pauwels van Hilligaert: *The Battle of Nieuwpoort*

Cornelis Vroom: *Battle on the Haarlemmer Meer*, 1629

In the decades before Vermeer was born, the Dutch commemorated in pictures the events that for so long had tried their courage. A center of resistance during the 80-year struggle with Spain was Haarlem, and the long siege which the town endured is the subject of the painting above and of the etching at right. Attacked from both the land and sea by the Spaniards, the walled city managed to hold out for seven months until famine forced its surrender. "See here," begins the inscription under the engraving, "how the Spaniards press the people of Haarlem." In the foreground is the enemy encampment from which stream cavalrymen and soldiers; to the right, in front of the dunes, may be seen other troops. Most of the towers of the city have already been shot down and a breach has been made in the wall. And off the coast ships are engaged in battle.

The Spaniards came to Haarlem on a route of destruction. First they plundered Mechelen; then they stormed Zutphen and slaughtered almost all of its citizens; next they conquered Naarden. When at last they entered Haarlem, they took 300 of the defenders, tied them and tossed them into the water to drown. Yet even in defeat, assaulted by "stench and atrocities," the inhabitants clung to their pride. "You have broken the Spanish Army before your town," the inscription says, trumpeting the moral victory Haarlem had thus won, "and given the whole country a secure faith."

TBELEG VAN HÆRLEM

W. Akersloot sculpt

hebt den Spaenschen arm voor u we Stad gebroken,
rome Bataviers! en synen trotz geyroken
n'tgantsche Vaderland een seker heyl bereyd.
ie krone komt ú toe voor uwe dapperheyd!

Gy weet wat Spanjen is, en wat wy daer verwachten,
Graveert dat in uw hert, en houd't het in gedachten
Doet als gy hebt gedaen, en sterkt uw moed, en hand,
En offert goed en bloed voor God, en 't vaderland.

Willem Akersloot: *The Siege of Haarlem*, c. 1628

Bartholomeus van der Helst: *The Banquet of the Civic Guard, June 18th, 1648, to Celebrate the Peace of Münster*, 1648

Willem van de Velde the Elder: *The Battle of the Downs, 1639*, 1659

The death blow to Spanish power in The Netherlands came in 1639 when Vermeer was seven. In the famous Battle of the Downs (so named because it was fought in waters just off the British coastal district of that name, while a squadron of English ships looked helplessly on) the Dutch Admiral Marten Harpertszoon Tromp annihilated the Spanish fleet. To the Dutch, his victory seemed all the greater because of the fantastic odds—Tromp had only 13 ships at his command as opposed to the 77 ships and 20,000 men of the Spaniards. Nor was this all—the Dutchmen practically had to cajole the enemy into fighting.

The detail above, from a large pen-and-ink drawing by Willem van de Velde the Elder, one of Holland's greatest sea artists, shows a Spanish flagship at far left on fire.

When peace became fact nine years later with the signing of the Treaty of Münster, the Dutch seemed well prepared for it—just how well prepared is suggested by the painting at left. It shows the Amsterdam Civic Guard, or militia, celebrating the Treaty of Münster with a banquet. Not only had its members grown rich and easygoing in the intervening years but also, from the jowly look of their flushed faces, impressively stout.

A major source of tiny Holland's prosperity was its overseas trade. Long before the Treaty of Münster brought peace, the Dutch had extended their commercial activities beyond the boundaries of Europe "to distant and exotic lands, as far as shines the sun." Their determination to achieve a monopoly in spices had led to the seizure and destruction of the Javanese port of Jakarta and the erection of a walled city at Batavia. And their desire "to keep the cooking going in the kitchens of the fatherland" through control of other Asian markets

put their ships off the coast of China and their merchants ashore even in insular Japan—a foothold they would keep, to the exclusion of all other Westerners, until 1854. In the detail from the Japanese scroll below, two Dutchmen wearing pantaloons honor a Japanese guest with food and music at their agency in Deshima, an island-enclave off Nagasaki. Dutch policy elsewhere tended to be less polite. It was characterized by a cold determination, out of which came a commercial empire greater than Portugal's and a rival to Spain's.

A Dutch Factory at Deshima, Nagasaki, detail, c. 1690

During the years of Vermeer's early childhood, all Holland seemed possessed, and the cause of its madness was a strange, new flower, recently introduced from Turkey, the tulip. Money could be made breeding variegated and striped types like those depicted here, and anyone so lucky as to own a mutation could expect to collect a fortune for it. One tulip fancier actually exchanged a thousand pounds of cheese, four oxen, eight pigs, 12 sheep, a bed and a suit of clothes, among other things, for a single bulb of the Viceroy at top right. Wild

Attributed to Crispin van der Passe the Younger: *Flora Leading the Tulip Speculators to Destruction* (date unknown)

speculation broke out, and, as the engraving below suggests, many Dutchmen were lured by the promise of profit into making foolish investments. Sitting in a wheeled sailing car labeled "The Fool's Wagon" is Flora, attended by such good-for-nothing types as Eager Rich and Idle Hope. Following behind is a crowd of simple people, who, in their haste to climb on board, have trampled underfoot the very means of their livelihood. When the bottom fell out of the tulip market, as it did in 1637, the entire Dutch economy rocked.

The Princess, 1643

Viceroy, 1643

Landscape of Berings and *La Vene,* 1643

Semper Augustus, 1643

Admiral van der Eyck, 1643

Purple and White Jerome, 1643

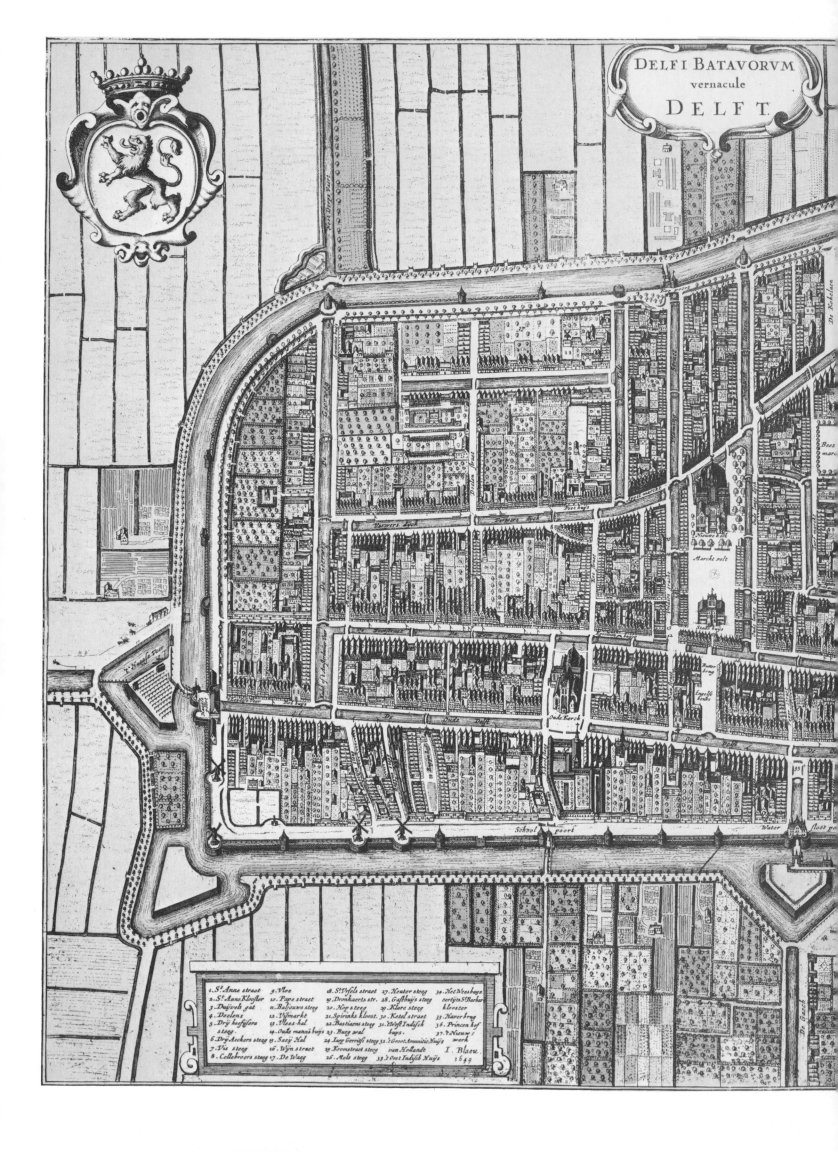

DELFI BATAVORVM vernacule DELFT.

1. St Anne straet	9. Vloe	18. St Vfels straet	27. Keuter steeg	34. Het Weeshuys
2. St Anne Klooster	10. Pape straet	19. Dronkaerts str.	28. Gasthuys steeg	eertijts St Barbar
3. Duyvels gat	11. Baljouws steeg	20. Kop steeg	29. Klare steeg	klooster
4. Doelens	12. Vismarkt	21. Spirinks kloost.	30. Ketel straet	35. Naver brug
5. Dry hoefijsers steeg	13. Vlees hal	22. Bastiaens steeg	31. t Weft Indisch huys	36. Princen hof
6. Dry Aeckers steeg	14. Oude manns huys	23. Burg wal	32. t Groot Amunitie Huys	37. t Nieuw werk
7. Vis steeg	15. Saey Hal	24. Jacq Gerritfs steeg	van Hollandt	
8. Cellebroers steeg	16. Wyn straet	25. Kromstraet steeg	33. t Oost Indisch Huys	I. Blaeu.
	17. De Waeg	26. Mols steeg		1649

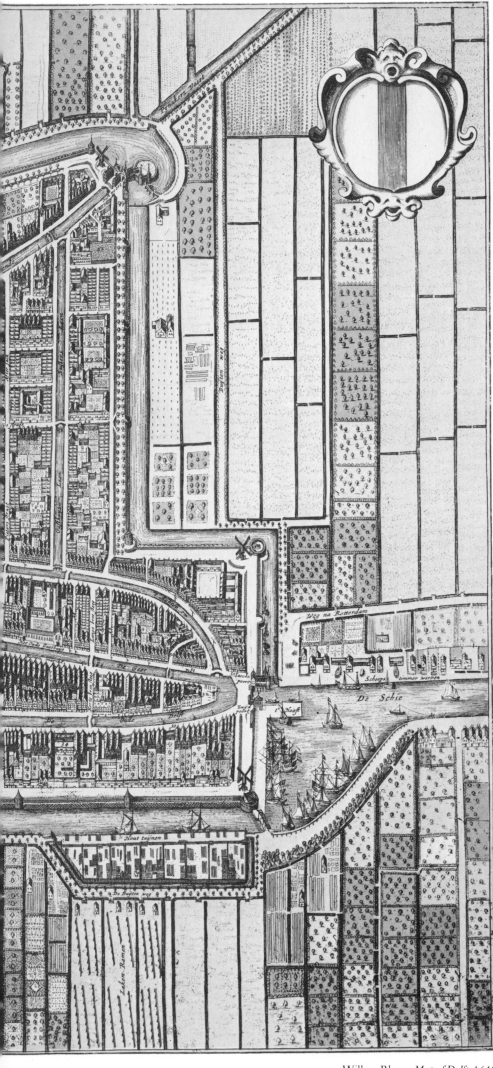

Engraved maps, like this one of Vermeer's home town of Delft by the great cartographer Willem Blaeu, enjoyed a vogue in Holland during the 17th Century. A reason for their popularity must have been their detail. Here may be seen many sites connected with Vermeer, including his house on the market square at the center of town, to the left of the church and just below the row of trees.

Delft was not much different in appearance from any other 17th Century Dutch town of its size, ringed by walls and crisscrossed by canals; but on October 12, 1654, at half past 10 in the morning, an event occurred to set it apart forever in the minds of Vermeer's contemporaries. The gunpowder magazine, jammed with explosives left over from the Spanish war and located in the upper left-hand corner of the town, blew up, sweeping away "whole families . . . even streets with people." When the smoke and gases had cleared and the dust had settled, all that marked the spot where the magazine had been was a pool of water 15 to 16 feet deep. Trees had been leveled to the ground, more than 200 houses destroyed, another 300 left roofless and windowless. Of those that escaped severe damage, many had "the furniture spoiled, all the china broken." The force of the blast buckled even the stout walls of the New Church diagonally opposite Vermeer's house, Mechelen.

Willem Blaeu: *Map of Delft*, 1649

De STICHTERS VANDIT WERK·
ZYNDEE SEMETHAAR VIEREN·
WIENSWAAPENSMETHAARNAAM·
DOENDEESEMUIER VERSIEREN·
ANNO 1737

IOH·TICHELAAR·   IAN·STEENSMA·   HEROD·IAGER·   WYBE·STEENSMA·

Pottery factory at Bolsward, Friesland, 1737

Delft teapot, c. 1680-1692

One of the important industries of Delft was the manufacture of earthenware —Delftware, as it is called. Pottery workshops abounded, producing everything from such elaborate imitations of Chinese porcelain as this teapot and vase to the humble and ubiquitous wall tiles which can be seen in several of Vermeer's paintings. The view of the tile factory opposite is itself composed of tiles, 154 of them, and illustrates how pottery was made. At the bottom level, workers stoke the kiln as horses turn mills grinding pigments and minerals for glazes; in an antechamber artists paint designs on pieces to be fired. At the second level, other craftsmen turn dishes on potter's wheels; and at the third level, workmen cut out tiles from slabs of clay.

The overseas expansion of the Dutch affected the pottery industry in many ways. The importation of millions of pieces of Chinese porcelain between 1602 and 1657 spurred the native manufacturers of earthenware to copy—and improvise on —Oriental designs. One critic has gone so far as to say that the enamel-smooth finish of Vermeer's paintings, his unusual and delicate color harmonies and even his delight in subtle ornamentation may reflect the influence upon him of the potter's art.

Delft vase, 1691

If a single painting can be said to summon up—and sum up—an entire age, it is perhaps this one, Vermeer's famous *View of Delft*. It not only shows exactly what a Dutch town of the 17th Century looked like; it also catches a moment of time, and in so doing delivers to all time a living relic of that century, with clouds moving slowly overhead and sunshine sparkling along the edges of red-tile rooftops.

In the precision of its detail the *View of Delft* does something else as well: it reflects the concern of the 17th Century Dutch with reality, with a world that could be seen—and explained. There is a clarity about the painting, as though a sudden rain had cleansed the air and left raindrops gleaming in the cracks and crevices of the buildings' brick façades. The light that pours down out of the towering sky is real light, peculiarly Dutch in its liquid character. But it can also be considered, as Descartes might have said, to be yet one more manifestation of "the natural light of the mind." Vermeer, as thoughtful an artist as any, after all, created it with his paint.

View of Delft

III

Man of Delft

Delft was the third city of Holland to receive a municipal charter—in 1246—and it remained in the forefront of Dutch history for several centuries. As well as being a center of resistance and headquarters for William of Orange during the war with Spain, it was the birthplace of some of the new nation's proudest figures: the Admirals Piet Hein and Marten Harpertzoon Tromp; Prince Frederick Henry, son of William and one of the war's military heroes; Hugo Grotius, jurist and statesman who established the principles of international law; scientist Anton van Leeuwenhoek, one of the first microbiologists. When Holland began to flourish in the late 16th Century, Delft shared the new prosperity.

Then in the second half of the 17th Century (about the time Vermeer's career was beginning) as Amsterdam and Rotterdam, because of their excellent ports, took over more and more of the nation's trade, Delft slowed down. Its famous pottery industry continued to flourish, but other businesses languished. The number of breweries in the city shrank from more than 100 to 15. It became the home of retired people and a stronghold of conservative Calvinism. Gradually the once-vigorous city went into a decline that left it virtually dormant until the 19th Century.

The one lucky result of this misfortune is that the heart of Delft today looks very much as it did in Vermeer's day, since, by the time the town came to life again, men had learned to value and preserve the architectural heritage of the past. Thus Delft still has a few acres of houses, churches, canals and squares which lead us straight into Vermeer's world. In fact, a plan of Delft, published in 1648 by the map maker Willem Blaeu, so detailed that it shows Vermeer's house, is accurate enough to be used for a walk today *(pages 50-51)*.

The center of old Delft is the market, which is shown as a white oblong in the middle of Blaeu's plan. The market square is not particularly large, but it is dramatic because it is the only wide-open, ornamental space within a medieval huddle of houses. Old Delft, which had about 23,000 inhabitants in 1630, actually boasts only three or four real streets; the rest are alleys and canals. The canals were the arteries of Delft, carrying its trade and also its visitors; in fact, Holland's waterways

This view from the back window of his home shows how acute Vermeer's powers of observation were. The three women, the alley, the houses, the bricks, are rendered with a precision that sidesteps finicky detail yet conveys a powerful impression of reality.

Street in Delft

were its safest and smoothest channels of transportation until well into the 19th Century. Marcel Proust described one such waterway after visiting Delft: "An ingenious little canal . . . dazzled by the pale sunlight; it ran between a double row of trees stripped of their leaves by summer's end and stroking with their branches the mirroring windows of the gabled houses on either bank."

Now these narrow canals lie quiet under their humpbacked bridges, but they are still used to carry supplies to the flower market, the butter-and-cheese market and the fish market, all located along the waterside. They are almost straight, but their slight bends provide surprising changes in the fall of the light, which is confined by the houses, reflected in windows and water and sifted through the canopy of the trees.

The light of Delft! Thousands of words have been written about it and its real or imagined secrets. The French playwright and poet Paul Claudel wrote that it was "the most beautiful light in existence." Considered coldly, there is no reason why the light of Delft should be different from the light of The Hague or Rotterdam. But the old town is so still, even today—the heavy foliage, the dark water and the old brick walls envelop it so beautifully—that its light, many times reflected and filtered, does seem different once it has reached the level of the eye; it seems to have an especially soft, fluid quality.

Perhaps it is not only Delft, not just the trees or canals, which make this light so special, but also Vermeer. As Stratford-on-Avon or Walden Pond may move the visitor in a manner which has nothing to do with their physical appearances, so the light of Vermeer's town has been given a magical connotation by his work.

Here he was born in the autumn of the year 1632. The first time his name is mentioned is in the baptismal register of the New Church, which stands on the east side of the market square. The entry for October 31 mentions the baptism of the child Joannes, son of Reynier Janszoon and Dingnum Balthasars. That century was less precise with names than we are now; it is only through comparison with other documents that we know that Reynier Janszoon—that is, Reynier, Jan's son—was Vermeer's father and Dymphna (not Dingnum), daughter of Balthasar, was his mother. Reynier's family name was actually Vos, and only when young Vermeer was about 20 did his father start calling and signing himself "Reynier Jansz. Vos, alias Vermeer" (or, on occasion, van der Meer). His reasons for this change are unknown. The name of the child, Joannes, is also written Johannes; it is the equivalent of the English John and in Holland it is usually abbreviated to Jan, or sometimes to Hans.

Reynier Janszoon and his wife had been married 17 years when Johannes, their second child, was born. They had to walk only a few hundred feet to the church for the baptism, for their own house, called "Mechelen," faced the same market square, on the north side. Mechelen was a busy establishment, for here Reynier kept a tavern and also designed and sold *caffa,* a kind of silk cloth. This last activity had become his main source of income by the time Jan was born. But Reynier was also an art dealer, and in 1631, the year before Jan's birth, the Guild of St. Luke had registered him as Master Art-Dealer, an essential requirement in a society where all vocations involving the arts were strictly guild-regulated.

The next time Jan Vermeer's name is mentioned, he is 20 years old. On April 5, 1653, the marriage register of the Town Hall records the wedding of "Johannes Vermeer, son of Reynier, bachelor, on the Market Square, with Catharina Bolnes, spinster, of the same place." Vermeer and his new bride lived with his parents in Mechelen and there they stayed most of their married life—until 1672, when they moved to a smaller house. There is not a word in writing about Vermeer's youth; it is known that his wife came from a prosperous family of nearby Gouda, and that she was a year older than he.

Less than a year after his marriage, on December 29, 1653, Jan Vermeer was enrolled as Master-Painter in the Guild of St. Luke. This was a crucial date in any artist's life, and it suggests that Vermeer must have worked as a painter's apprentice from about 1647, when he was 15, since six or seven years was the time required to become a master.

The Royal Library in The Hague still has the Guild Book of those years—a long, thin book in a parchment cover. Its records go up to 1714 and, besides painters, list the names of the sculptors, booksellers, potters, art dealers, stonecutters, tapestry weavers and glass painters of Delft, all members of the Guild of St. Luke. It is moving to look up Vermeer's registration and find that of the six-guilder initiation fee required of a citizen of Delft only one guilder and ten stiver were paid at the time of his acceptance. In the margin of the same page in the Guild Book we find written, "On July 24, 1656, all was paid."

Thus it was two and a half years before Vermeer paid his remaining debt of four guilders and ten stiver, which may give some indication of the financial circumstances of the newly married couple. (The value of the 17th Century guilder is very hard to determine in terms of today's money. Its buying power was probably the equivalent of four dollars. Thus, Vermeer's six-guilder initiation fee amounted to about 24 dollars. The stiver is a Dutch nickel; there were 20 to the guilder.)

Vermeer joined his father in the art dealership, but the partnership did not last long. The elder Vermeer died in 1655. His widow continued to live in Mechelen with the young couple, who by that time must have had the first of the 11 children they were to have over the next 20 years.

Some scholars have devoted considerable research to Vermeer's religious convictions and have come up with evidence showing that he may have been Roman Catholic. His parents probably were not, although his baptism in the Protestant New Church is no clear proof of that: Catholicism was not fully tolerated in Holland, and purely Catholic services were performed only in private. Moreover, since there were no Catholic churches, many Catholics were buried in Protestant church cemeteries. Vermeer's wife, Catharina, was from a Catholic family, and it is likely that he agreed to have their children taught the Catholic catechism.

If Vermeer did become a convinced Catholic, it could have some bearing on a certain trend toward mysticism in his work—but the argument may be turned around as easily by assuming that the mysticism was there and that it made him more sympathetic to Catholicism.

Among the few existing documents relating to Vermeer's life is the registration book of the Guild of St. Luke, the painters' union. On the page above, Vermeer's signature can be seen opposite the number 78; it was partly crossed out, probably at his death in 1675. Carel Fabritius, Vermeer's supposed teacher, signed at number 75 and the word *doot* (dead) has been added after his name. At number 80 is the signature of Pieter de Hoogh, a successful contemporary.

Whatever the merits of these arguments, it seems clear, judging from his paintings, that Vermeer was not a dogmatic or narrowly theological man. Sniffing through old papers for more proof of his religion may be interesting historical detective work, but it has little bearing on our understanding of him as an artist.

We know nothing of Vermeer's artistic apprenticeship, or of who his teacher was, and almost nothing of his reputation in Delft. But his career did start with something of a flourish. This is attested by the only piece of contemporary public praise of him as an artist that has been discovered. It came in 1654, the year after his marriage, when Delft was struck by a terrible calamity: the gunpowder magazine, containing some 80,000 or 90,000 pounds of powder, blew up "with such a horrible rush and force," as a contemporary account states, "that the arch of heaven seemed to crack and to burst." The explosion was heard all the way to "the North Sea and in some provinces outside Holland." It killed hundreds of people and did great damage to at least half the buildings of the town, including the great New Church, which stood across the street from Mechelen.

One of the victims of the "Delft Thunderclap" was the painter Carel Fabritius, who was buried under the ruins of his house, together with his family and a man sitting for his portrait. The artist's death led a Delft publisher to compose a memorial poem, the last verse of which mourns the loss of the brilliant Fabritius, but also mentions Vermeer:

> *Thus this Phoenix was extinguished,*
> *To our loss, at the height of his power.*
> *But happily there arose from his fire*
> *Vermeer, who followed in his footsteps with mastery.*

It has been tempting to deduce from these lines that Vermeer was a pupil of Fabritius. Undoubtedly, certain similarities in the two artists' work—for example, the play of light and the use of light-colored backgrounds—indicate a strong influence on Vermeer by the older Fabritius; but there is no tangible proof that Vermeer studied with him.

Still, if we cannot discover who Vermeer's teacher was during his apprentice years, we can gather an impression of the esthetic influences and artistic traditions that must have affected him during that formative period in his life.

In the Old Church of Delft the only important art left by the war and the anti-Papist demonstrations had been its Gothic stained-glass windows. (They were later shattered by the gunpowder magazine explosion.) The Old Church also had a beautifully executed pulpit with 16th Century wood carvings. There were new funeral monuments for famous men in both the New and Old Churches—for Admiral Piet Hein, for instance, and for Prince William of Orange, by Hendrick de Keyser—but they were executed in a pompous baroque style, which must have left Jan Vermeer as cold as the marble they were made of.

The Town Hall, completed in 1620, was an architectural gem in the Northern Renaissance style (19th Century changes have spoiled its lines considerably). The Gemeenlandshuis, a private residence which is still standing, was even in Vermeer's time the finest surviving specimen of early 16th Century Gothic architecture.

Inside the Town Hall, the walls were covered with tapestries up to about two thirds of their height. These were woven in Dutch and Flemish workshops and showed considerable artistic merit and they may well have fascinated the young Vermeer. Probably not so interesting to him was a series of portraits by Michiel van Miereveld, showing William, Prince of Orange, and his successors. Although Van Miereveld was the leading painter of what little there was left in the United Provinces of traditional "court art," there is little in Vermeer's paintings to suggest he found any inspiration in the Van Miereveld canvases.

Much more important in influencing Vermeer during his early years were the paintings his father handled as an art dealer, as well as the works he could see in the studios of the artists of Delft. We have seen how Holland's painters separated themselves from the mainstream of European Catholic art; they were to be realists. But such breaks in art history are never total. The great prestige of Italy was still alive and Dutch artists still maintained contact with the wellspring of European art.

Caravaggio and the style that art historians have dubbed "Caravaggism" helped bridge this gap. Caravaggio, whose given name was Michelangelo Merisi, was a rebellious young North Italian painter who, toward the end of the 16th Century, introduced a new kind of realism into Italian art; eventually the movement inspired by his influence spread to at least two generations of Flemish, Spanish, French and Dutch painters.

By breaking away from the idealization of form and subject of late Renaissance painting, Caravaggism introduced a new way of looking at the world and representing it on canvas. A painter could now paint what he saw in the world around him, often retaining traditional religious and mythological themes but casting them in everyday settings. Mary Magdalene, for example, was now shown as a simple serving girl rather than

Delft's devastation in 1654, caused by the accidental explosion of some 80,000 pounds of gunpowder in the town's arsenal, is shown in a painting by Egbert van der Poel. Carel Fabritius died in the wreckage. Vermeer's house, close to the New Church, whose spire is seen at far left, probably suffered damage.

as an idealized beauty. Caravaggio had also been the first of his generation to experiment with dramatic effects of light in his paintings, making
bold use of contrasting highlights and shadow to set off his subjects—a
method that was to find its most highly refined expression in the Dutch
painting of the Golden Age.

Many Dutch painters went to Italy at this time to study and work,
and they found Caravaggio's new realism highly congenial to their own
traditions; his work strongly influenced their own. When they returned
to Holland, most of them settled in Utrecht, a largely Catholic city with
close ties to Rome. Here the School of Utrecht flourished and the Italianate paintings that came from its studios were very much in the public eye, and were therefore well represented in the art dealers' salons.
Without doubt, many of the paintings which were bought and sold by
the Vermeers, father and son, were from the Utrecht School. Vermeer's
work shows that he saw them and learned from them and that he then
traveled much further along the road of realism.

In Delft itself there were many artists whose work must have influenced Vermeer's development. Leonard Bramer had gone to study in
Italy; returning from Rome, he settled in Delft in 1629 and, although
40 years older than Vermeer, became friends with him. His signature
is on Vermeer's marriage license as a witness and he was a member of
the Guild board with Vermeer in 1661. Among other notable painters
who also worked in Delft were Pieter de Hoogh, who lived there for
several years and was especially known for his domestic scenes; Paulus
Potter, a bright young painter of animal and landscape pictures; Emanuel
de Witte, preoccupied with problems of perspective and the play of
light on stone and brick in the churches of Delft; and, of course, Carel
Fabritius, who had been a pupil of Rembrandt, and whose career
might have been one of the most brilliant of his time had it not been
snuffed out by the great Delft Thunderclap.

All these men were members of the Guild of St. Luke, and probably
all of them lived within a dozen city blocks of one another; they must
have known one another very well indeed. Each must have seen the
others' work; without doubt they discussed it and quarreled over it
and reacted to it in a strongly personal and emotional way.

We do not know much more about Vermeer's artistic background.
One town chronicle tells us that in 1663 a carillon of 36 bells was in-
stalled in the New Church ("the latest thing," the chronicler writes).
Their music must have become a permanent enrichment in Vermeer's
life, who could hear them in his studio. Like many of his contemporary
artists, Vermeer seems to have been greatly interested in music and musical instruments, as his paintings show. In fact, these prove Vermeer's
general erudition: besides music, he touches in his work on mythology,
astronomy and geography.

The records tell of only one visit made by an art collector to Vermeer's
studio. The French nobleman Balthasar de Monconys, who went on a
scientific and art-collecting tour of the Lowlands in 1663, reports having
gone to see Vermeer at Mechelen. For reasons that are not clear, the
artist had none of his own paintings to show the visitor, but he sent him

to the shop of a baker who had a Vermeer painting for which he had paid 300 guilders. De Monconys obviously had different values from those of today's critics: he was astonished at the painting's 300-guilder cost and stated that he would not have paid more than 50 guilders for it, especially since it had only one figure in it. (It is impossible to tell which picture it was that De Monconys held in such low esteem.)

Despite the unenthusiastic reaction of this one collector, Vermeer was well enough respected by other contemporaries to be considered an expert in his field. In 1671, four years before his death, he adjudicated a dispute between an art dealer of Amsterdam and the Elector of Brandenburg. The latter had refused to pay an agreed sum of 30,000 guilders for a collection of Italian masters whose authenticity he doubted. The art dealer insisted they were genuine and took his case to the authorities. Vermeer and a fellow artist from Delft were called to The Hague to pass judgment; they studied the paintings and ruled decisively against the art dealer, declaring that the paintings "not only were not excellent Italian pictures but on the contrary did not deserve to bear the name of a good master." It is the only statement by Vermeer on the subject of art that we have in writing, but it reveals the temperament of a man of broad artistic knowledge and firm conviction.

The book that registers Vermeer's acceptance into the Guild of St. Luke also records that on two occasions, in 1662 and again in 1670, he served two-year terms on the board of the Guild. The practice was to elect six members; the first year three served as administrators and three as standbys; the following year they changed places. Thus, in 1663 and again in 1671, Vermeer held the job of dean of the Guild, which proves he was considered a serious citizen—although the job itself may well have involved more drudgery than prestige.

There is little else to be told. The only other data bearing on Vermeer's life are a number of notary acts concerning loans—those he contracted himself or, occasionally, loans of friends which he cosigned. (The Dutch kept meticulous records of all financial transactions, which explains why we know so much more about Vermeer's monetary affairs than his personal life.) In 1655 he borrowed 200 guilders; he repaid it with interest a year later. At about the same time, he assumed a debt of 250 guilders which his father had left unpaid at his death. The records of these few transactions suggest that Vermeer lived a frugal life.

Sadly enough, his financial condition deteriorated at the end. In 1672 the Vermeers gave up the tavern business, rented Mechelen to a tenant and moved to a smaller house. By the time he died in 1675, there was nothing left. His widow petitioned the town council for a bankruptcy ruling and for financial help with the education of her children.

But if he left no money, he did leave his life's work—between 30 and 40 paintings, which were to be buffeted about among his various creditors, the executor of his estate and his widow, who waged a brave struggle to keep at least some of them in her possession. These paintings now represent an incalculable treasure, and they also—as we will see—reveal fully as much about Vermeer, the unknown, as do the few existing records that document his everyday life in Delft.

When Jan Vermeer signed his name to *The Procuress* *(opposite)*, one of his earliest known paintings, he was 24, newly married, just starting out on his career. Presumably, since it was close to the sources from which his first inspiration had come, the painting should have much to tell about the formative influences on Vermeer. But as with so much else that he did, it is strangely unrevealing—a minor masterpiece that seems to have sprung ready-made from his imagination. Practically all it says with any certainty is that from the start Vermeer was, at least in his choice of themes, very much a man of his times. The lusty subject he handled here had long been a favorite of Dutch artists.

What were the influences on Vermeer? Certainly he did not grow up in a vacuum; he belonged to the last generation of painters of the Golden Age, and behind him already lay many of the great achievements in Dutch art. And yet his approach to his subject matter was so different as to seem without precedent. Whose paintings did he see as an art dealer in Delft and as a leading member of its artists' guild? How did he arrive at his unique vision of the world as space drenched in light and color? Tantalized by questions like these, art scholars have taken another look at 17th Century painters of light —and in doing so, they have uncovered not only some possible sources for Vermeer's inspiration but also some neglected artists whose reputations deserve refurbishing.

Masters and Mentors

Approaching mastery, but not yet a master, the young Vermeer apparently had difficulty working out the perspective in this painting. He seems to have been looking down at the table and up at the girl at the same time —a visual impossibility. The laughing figure at far left may be a self-portrait.

The Procuress, 1656

Revolting against all that he deemed mannered and stiffly artificial in Post-Renaissance Italian art, the deeply emotional painter Caravaggio daringly portrayed the real world in his works. Even his models were real people, like this gypsy who pretends to tell a young man's fortune while slipping off his ring.

Caravaggio: *The Fortune Teller*, c. 1595

Gerrit van Honthorst: *The Procuress*, 1625

Though time and distance separated him widely from the emergent art of Holland, the Italian painter Michelangelo Merisi da Caravaggio nonetheless exerted a decisive influence on all of European painting in the 17th Century. His spirit is plain in the works shown here by three leading figures in the School of Utrecht—Hendrick Terbrugghen, Gerrit van Honthorst and Dirck van Baburen. They helped disseminate through their paintings their own peculiarly northern interpretation of Caravaggio's realism. Although the master's interest in light was retained, Dutch intimacy replaced Italian monumentality, and the dramatic gave way to genre.

Vermeer had in his home at least one painting by a member of the Utrecht School—the Baburen at right. His *Procuress* was painted on the same theme of venal love, and the flicker of candlelight in it (his only known use of the Caravaggio-inspired artificial lighting) may indicate a connection to Utrecht during his formative years. But perhaps his subtlest—and at the same time strongest—link to the school is through the late works of Terbrugghen, in which the light has something of the soft glow, the daylight tone, of Vermeer himself.

Dirck van Baburen: *The Procuress*, 1622

Hendrick Terbrugghen: *Scene of Mercenary Love*, c. 1627

Pieter Saenredam: *Interior of St. Lawrence's Church at Alkmaar*, 1661

As the Utrecht painters used light to heighten the effect of their paintings, so other Dutch artists made it in large measure the subject of their art. Within Vermeer's own town of Delft, there were several painters of light. One of these was Emanuel de Witte, a misanthropic atheist whose intellectual pleasure nevertheless was depicting the insides of churches. Among his masterpieces is the radiant painting at right. Still another Dutch painter of light was Pieter Saenredam of Haarlem, a hunchback who, like De Witte, concerned himself almost exclusively with church interiors and again for much the same reason—because they were open places where light fell through clear glass windows onto clean white walls. In the work below, however, he has added a personal detail, the tomb of his father.

The works of Saenredam and De Witte came as close to being pure painting as any in the 17th Century, with one obvious exception—the canvases of Vermeer himself. Like Vermeer, neither artist had a story to tell, and both subordinated people to the overall effect, using them often only for scale. Light was the all-important ingredient, and through the use of brilliant yet subtle techniques, each man captured it in the very act of hollowing out space.

Emanuel de Witte: *Interior of a Church*, c. 1680

Pieter Saenredam: *Interior of St. Odulphus' Church at Assendelft*, 1649

Carel Fabritius: *The Goldfinch*, 1654

Who was Vermeer's teacher? The question will probably never be answered with any finality. The man most often suggested is Carel Fabritius, the brilliant and promising young painter who was killed in the Delft gunpowder explosion the very year that Vermeer became a member of the artists' guild.

The qualities that link Fabritius to Vermeer shine out from the works reproduced here. In both paintings, a figure is displayed against a light, glowing background, and in both space has been so skillfully handled that an almost three-dimensional effect results. But there is something else here suggestive of Vermeer: the choice of a simple subject with a concentrated inner meaning. The bird seated upon the perch of the seed box would seem to be an ordinary bird, a household pet, but it is in fact a goldfinch, whose predilection for thorns and thistles linked it to Christ's Passion—and which for that reason made it a symbol of the Passion. Similarly, the sentinel asleep in the painting opposite would seem to be just another genre subject, but Fabritius has introduced enough symbols to show that he intended his 17th Century viewers to draw a moral lesson from the picture. The guard is attended by a dog, an animal traditionally associated with watchfulness and fidelity—virtues the guard obviously lacks. On the plaque above the arch can be seen the figure of St. Anthony Abbot. The saint serves as a clue to the sentinel's downfall, for it was he who overcame temptation by fasting, praying and chastising the flesh. It is the guard's failure to follow the saint's example that has made him completely useless on the job.

Carel Fabritius: *The Sentinel*, 1654

IV

The Pioneers

Jan Vermeer and his contemporaries were in the last generation of Dutch painters who produced the brilliant art of the 17th Century. Before them came a group of artists who pioneered in developing the extraordinary skills that were the glory of the Golden Age.

The first great figure of these early years was Frans Hals. His parents settled in Haarlem in 1591 when Hals was about 10, and here he spent his long and immensely active life; here he died in 1666. His first group portrait—one of those for which he is so famous—was done in 1616: *The Officers of the Archers of St. George* shows a banquet of the dashing members of a unit of the civic guard. In it the essence of his mature style—his free technique of rapid, easy brushstrokes—is already evident. For Hals this technique was not an end in itself but was a means of achieving an effect of effortlessness and spontaneity that was to change the very nature of portrait painting. (Almost 300 years later Vincent van Gogh expressed particular admiration for Hals's "way of stating the subject right away in one sweep.")

Hals's subjects shed the traditional, almost frozen, dignity of people sitting for portraits; instead, they are caught in a quick movement, in a moment of thought, in an ephemeral instant of laughter *(opposite)*. Thus the painter penetrates deeply into their real personalities. Brushstroke fits next to brushstroke, color is neighbor to different color without transition; there is no trace of drawing here—this is pure painting. But the effortlessness is only apparent, for nothing would be further from the truth than to imagine Frans Hals looking at his subject and then dashing down his paint without any additional thought. Close inspection of his work discloses a superb balance, a fine structure; it is Hals's virtuosity which makes it all seem so simple.

Like so many other Dutch painters, Hals found it paid to specialize. Though he showed great versatility in his work, his most reliable source of income was his large group portraits. Twelve of these have survived. They are striking for the genius with which the artist managed to satisfy his vain customers without sacrificing his integrity as a painter.

The most famous of these are the last two he painted; they show the

Board of Governors and the Board of Governesses of the Haarlem Old Men's Almshouse. Hals painted these at the end of his life, when he was over 80, and they show a remarkable perception and wisdom. They are virtually in monochrome; there is only the black of the costumes, the white lace collars and the light on the faces; in the painting of the women there is just one touch of red—on the pages of a book on a table in the foreground. It must be either the Bible or the accounts book of the Board, and the viewer feels that both these books were equally sacred in that place. These severe old men and women of the Board are shown so convincingly and with such simplicity, their loneliness and aloneness shining through so mysteriously, that it is not hard, looking at them, to understand why Hals earned a place among the great masters.

When he painted these last portraits—and indeed until his death—Hals was actually living on a few guilders a week voted to him by these same Governors and Governesses, his more than 50 years of work as a painter having failed to provide him with anything for his old age. For Hals in his personal life was nearly as undisciplined and exuberant as some of the boisterous soldiers and cavaliers he painted. A good number of the contemporary references to Hals come from the police records of Haarlem, which indicate he had an unquenchable enthusiasm for drinking and carousing. He had two wives and at least 12 children (the total is uncertain), and, though he was well thought of as an artist and received many commissions, he could never stay out of debt for long. When he finally died in his mid-eighties, he was a pauper—but he was given an honorable funeral in a Haarlem church.

However poorly Hals managed his private affairs, his artistic genius stayed intact to the end. He had an enormous influence on his colleagues and his pupils during these many years of work, and his painting not only lit the way brilliantly for the Dutch Golden Age, but was fresh and dynamic enough to be especially admired 200 years later by another band of pioneering artists, the Impressionists.

While Hals painted in Haarlem, a group of artists were marking a new course in Utrecht, a major town of the central Netherlands. These were the first Dutch painters to feel the impact of the Italian artistic revolution sparked by Caravaggio. Most of them had studied in Rome and there they were greatly influenced by Caravaggio's emphasis on reality—a reality that was set off dramatically, even theatrically, by bold colors, strong highlights and deep shadows. The painters of Utrecht took this style with them back to Holland, and it might be said that historically they were less important for their own paintings than for the influence they had on other Dutch painters—including, ultimately, Vermeer.

Gerrit van Honthorst, who lived between 1590 and 1656, was the chief liaison between Caravaggism and the painters of Holland. Although Caravaggio died about the time Honthorst arrived in Rome, the great Italian's principles were still being hotly debated and widely emulated; Honthorst quickly absorbed the message. He painted many night scenes of banquets and concerts, paying strict attention to realistic detail, using the definite colors that had marked Caravaggio's early works and showing a fascination for the lighting effects cast by torches and candles.

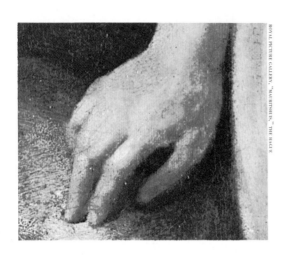

Frans Hals's vigorous brush technique was revolutionary in his day. The detail above shows the traditional style, in which a hand is modeled from smoothly stroked subtle colors. Hals's hand, below, is drawn in a few bold slashes of almost pure color, a technique that was to be revived, centuries later, by the rebellious French Impressionists.

Honthorst returned to Utrecht in 1621, and a painting such as his *Procuress (page 66),* done in 1625 when he was at the peak of his powers, shows how completely he had assimilated the two traditions of Holland and Italy. It is an intimate scene showing a young man flirting with a laughing girl while the procuress, an old crone, urges her on. The scene was to be painted many times by painters coming after Honthorst and is typical of Dutch genre painting; but Honthorst treats it in an Italianate manner, giving it a theatrical setting, dramatically lit by a candle in the direct tradition of Caravaggio.

Pictures such as this, as well as many showing joyous musicians, children or soldiers, introduced into the market place of Dutch art a new element of elegance combined with down-to-earth subject matter and made Honthorst fashionable overnight. An urbane, gregarious man, he became a favorite of King Charles I of England and of the Princes of Orange at The Hague; eventually he relinquished his position as an innovator of serious art—but ensured his financial position—when he turned to executing decorative paintings on the walls and ceilings of royal palaces and mansions.

A slightly older but less influential Utrecht colleague whose career closely paralleled Honthorst's was Hendrick Terbrugghen, born in 1588. Terbrugghen preceded Honthorst to Rome by a few years and he, too, spent about a decade there before returning to contribute to the popularity of Caravaggism at home. Like Honthorst, Terbrugghen painted musicians, boys smoking, girls of easy virtue *(page 67)*—all rendered in rich textures and colors. In demonstrating that no theme was too humble or trivial for the artist, the two painters, along with other members of the Utrecht School, contributed much to the secularization that was a dominant tendency of early 17th Century Dutch art.

But in many respects, Terbrugghen was very different from his fashionable associate. Deeply absorbed in his work, Terbrugghen was a retiring man who shunned the popularity Honthorst thrived on; records reveal only one instance when Terbrugghen painted a picture on commission. Artistically he was more refined than Honthorst. As he matured, Terbrugghen turned away from the brilliant, almost harsh colors of Italian painting and adopted a subtler, more subdued palette, while his rendering of the subject matter became gentler and more introspective. Indeed, his artistry was such that today he is considered the most accomplished painter of Utrecht. Even in his own day, though less famous than Honthorst, he enjoyed a considerable reputation: Rubens so admired his work that the great Flemish painter visited Terbrugghen's studio in Utrecht in 1627.

A third Utrecht painter is worth mentioning here not so much for his artistic merit, which today is judged to have been less than that of his better-known contemporaries, but because of an intriguing link between him and Vermeer. Dirck van Baburen, like other Utrecht artists, had gone to Rome and absorbed the Caravaggesque style. Like many other artists he painted several pictures on the theme of the procuress. Curiously, one of these paintings *(page 67)* appears in the background of two of Vermeer's masterpieces: the *Lady Seated at a Virginal* and *The*

Concert (page 156). In each case Vermeer changed the original's composition to suit his needs, but in each case his model was clearly the same Baburen *Procuress*.

Practically nothing is known of Vermeer's working habits and his own artistic taste, and it is tantalizing to speculate on why he should have twice picked this painting to include in his own pictures. Did he feel an affinity with Baburen's work? Did he find this particular *Procuress* among all the others especially well rendered? Or did he own the Baburen in his capacity as art dealer and simply use it as a thrifty expedient? From this distance in time little can be decided about the puzzle except that Vermeer's choice of the painting as a model indicates he must have had at least a professional admiration for the Utrecht artist.

The rise of Dutch landscape painting came at about the same time the School of Utrecht was flourishing, and the Dutch painters' fascination with the look of their land was to last throughout the Golden Age. It reached its finest expression, perhaps, in the work of Vermeer's contemporaries, but some of the earlier landscapists were masters in their own right: Hendrick Avercamp, Hercules Seghers, Jan van Goyen and Simon de Vlieger.

These men were pioneers in that branch of Dutch painting that was to be probably the most influential beyond the borders of the country; they were the chief precursors of the great English and French landscapists of the 19th Century. They also made a link with the painters of the Dutch past—the Van Eycks, Brueghel, Bosch—who, though their subjects were often allegorical, had dwelt lovingly in many pictures on the details of their countryside.

That Dutch countryside is oddly striking—it almost demands to be painted, although it has little of the drama of the tropics or of mountainous terrain. In fact, the land has almost no verticals at all but is conspicuously flat; the horizon is ever-present—so much so that the Dutch language has four words for horizon. The wind sweeps over the low land. The changeable sky, with its towering clouds reflected in rivers and canals, is more dramatic than the earth. Distance is emphasized not only by perspective but also by increasing haziness and a softening of faraway color. Rarely are contours sharp; often rain and sunshine alternate through the day. Nature itself seems as moody, as subjective, as man.

In their efforts to catch the essence of this ever-changing setting, the new landscapists painted pictures that were different from anything seen before. Nature was portrayed for its own sake rather than as a background to divine or human enterprises, or in an artificial arrangement to convey a literary allusion. The story element, though it was still evident in the earliest work of the period, later vanished completely. These artists painted the portraits, so to speak, of the trees, the rivers and the dunes. And as they did so, they learned to convey emotion not by using symbolic devices but by implying it in myriad subtle ways, through color, tone and composition. Their work mirrored nature, but in the end it also mirrored themselves.

Hendrick Avercamp, who was born in Amsterdam about 1585, loved to paint his country in the winter. He was enchanted by frozen, endless fields in gray winter light with perhaps just a touch of color from a flag on a barn; and by the peasants and townsmen as they engaged in the national winter pastime, skating *(page 94)*. The horizons are high up in these paintings, and the foregrounds are filled in with bright-colored figures. In his early work, Avercamp's detailed, anecdotal portrayal of daily life reminds us very strongly of Brueghel the Elder, except that Brueghel's vision often had a moody, almost supernatural cast, while Avercamp's was more cheerful.

Later, Avercamp's work became almost monochromatic: the mood, the tonality of the landscape override the local spots of color. At the same time, Avercamp lowered the horizons and made the dramatic Dutch sky, with its flying white and dark clouds, a vital element in the paintings.

Another early landscapist, whose work carried him in a different direction, was Hercules Seghers. It is known that he studied briefly in the same studio with Avercamp in Amsterdam during the early 1600s and later became a member of the St. Luke's Guild in Haarlem. Otherwise, little is known of Seghers' life. He was a somber, melancholy man who lived an isolated existence and whose work was appreciated by almost no one at the time, except Rembrandt. Rembrandt appears to have felt a kinship with Seghers. He owned eight of his paintings, and there is doubtless a relationship between the two artists' color schemes—both made extensive use of gray-greens and dark reddish browns contrasted against bright gold light.

Seghers carried the subjectivization of nature to an extreme which led him beyond the range of most Dutch landscapists: he turned his back on the actual scenes around him and painted landscapes which existed only in his troubled mind. In many of his paintings, and in his beautiful but rare color etchings, rocks rise on the left or on the right, sparsely covered with trees. In the center nothing halts the eye; there is only a far-away distance that in the mysterious and muted light seems the embodiment of all the loneliness in the world.

Jan van Goyen, one of Seghers' fellow members of the Haarlem St. Luke's Guild, was a few years younger and much more in the mainstream of Dutch landscapists. It is interesting to compare him with the two leading French landscapists of the day, Nicolas Poussin and Claude Lorrain. In their impeccably executed paintings, Poussin and Claude (as the latter is known) set a mood by their choice of subject: somber ruins, a bucolic scene of a young man playing a flute, tunic-clad shepherds deciphering the inscription on a tombstone in idyllic, picturesque surroundings. The very concept "picturesque" was born in these works, and rich country squires in France and England started to model their gardens in accordance with the French painters' romantic settings.

How different was Van Goyen! By the time he reached maturity as an artist—around 1640—Van Goyen had dropped all hints of anecdote, all obvious symbolic association from his paintings. His colors were simple, dominated by yellow and gray-green. His subjects were simple, too—peasant huts in the sand dunes, a distant town under a stormy sky, a beach or a view of the sea.

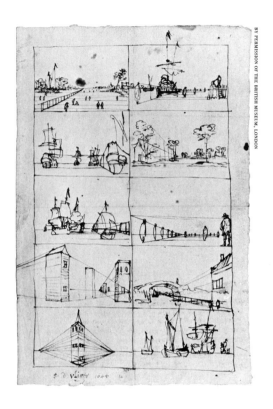

A sheet of studies by the seascapist Simon de Vlieger shows how he practiced sketching the proportions of various objects as they receded toward the horizon. Achieving both convincing perspectives and interesting compositions was especially difficult for Dutch outdoor painters, who faced an unremittingly flat land.

These quiet landscape paintings were often built around a river, dune or dike running in a strong diagonal across the picture, dividing the foggy land from a vast sky full of slow-moving clouds *(pages 114-115)*. Van Goyen made beautiful use of "aerial perspective." That is, he gradually diminished the intensity of the colors of the sky and land to give a sense of great distance; in fact, some of his work seems at first glance to be almost devoid of color. With this subdued expression he learned to convey emotion and mood in a way that is subtle and indirect, but eloquent.

Of course Holland is not just land and sky. There is also the ever-present sea—a source of wealth and at the same time a constant threat to a dike-rimmed land, a fruitful friend and an unforgiving foe. For Dutchmen the sea has always been part of life itself and Dutch landscape painters have long shared this preoccupation.

The first of many 17th Century artists to concentrate on capturing the sea's varied moods and humors was Simon de Vlieger, born in 1601. De Vlieger is an example of the painter forced into extreme specialization; although he was a man of many-sided talent who left some beautiful etchings of animals and forest scenes, he is known primarily for his pictures of beaches, naval battles and storms at sea.

Almost every Dutch seascape, from De Vlieger till the end of the era, contains at least one ship—as though it were unthinkable that there should be any stretch of salt water without a Dutch ship on it. In rendering the ships in his scenes, De Vlieger paid such attention to detail that experts still use his paintings to study the tackle and naval armament of that great age of Dutch and British seafaring.

If the landscapists were enchanted by the look of the land and sea, the genre painters were concerned with the people of the land. It should be remembered that in the years described here, painting had only recently abandoned its tradition as an art designed to inspire the onlooker with religious awe. The transition from that point of view to courtly art—art for the greater glory of a ruling prince—was not too drastic. But the step to genre, to the art of the everyday, had been more difficult.

The early 17th Century Dutch artists still hesitated to paint unadorned views of daily life—of a woman sewing, or even of just a room, an alleyway or a canal. They still felt that a painting needed more substance, and so they mixed up anecdote and hidden allegory: a sleeping servant girl subtly underlined the wickedness of sloth; a peasants' knife fight in a tavern was an indirect comment on the evils of drink. In this the artists were usually in good taste, and seldom sank to the sentimentality of some 18th and 19th Century genre. And soon, the best of them learned that anecdote was not really necessary to their work. Beauty was to be found everywhere, and it was the painting that counted, not the subject.

Adriaen Brouwer was one of the most intriguing personalities in the early generation of genre painters. He was born in the southern Lowlands about 1605, and he died, deeply in debt, in Antwerp at the age of 32. He worked in Haarlem, where he was influenced by Frans Hals, but during most of his short life he was a wanderer, a rollicking free spirit whose intrepid individualism made him the hero of many a legendary escapade. He is said to have once been captured by pirates; he was briefly

A lusty love of life pervades the work of Adriaen Brouwer whose painting *The Smokers (above)* recalls the practical jokes of his youth. He shows himself *(center)* about to get a "hot seat" from the prankster at left, while his elegant friend Jan Davidsz. de Heem and two amused rogues look on.

imprisoned by Spanish soldiers in 1633 for reasons unknown; he is believed to have served as a secret diplomat between the Republic and the Spanish governors still ruling the southern Lowlands from Antwerp.

As an artist Brouwer resembled the stereotype painter of more modern times: always penniless, often an outcast. He took pleasure in depicting not the serene domesticity of the burghers but the raw life of the lowly country taverns and smoking dens where peasants got "tobacco drunk" on pipefuls of tobacco doctored (possibly with locally grown hemp) to produce a narcotic effect *(page 92)*.

These harsh tableaux, executed with great attention to detail, showed the people almost in caricature and seemed to emphasize their low pleasures and unsavory habits. But the scenes are rendered in soft grays, browns and chiaroscuro, enriched by masterful strokes of subtle coloring. Brouwer's paintings were usually small in dimension—many of them were smaller than a page of this book—but they had great impact on his contemporaries, and they still have impact today.

One of those contemporaries was Adriaen van Ostade, who lived all his life in Haarlem, where in 1633 he became a member of the Guild at age 23. His work shows an abundance of peasants' inns and huts, emphasizing their dark interiors in gray, green, light blue and purple tones, with the light usually falling from an invisible source. Men and women are seen smoking and drinking, while often a local fiddler plays *(pages 90-91)*—all very much in the fashion of Brouwer but with less emphasis on the ugliness and rawness of life.

Unlike Brouwer and Ostade in his choice of subject matter was Gerard Dou, who lived from 1613 to 1675. With Dou (who was Rembrandt's earliest pupil in Leiden from 1628 until 1631), genre painting reached an almost microscopic refinement.

Dou painted gentle views of middle-class domesticity, rather than rowdy low-life scenes. On his small panels, Dou seems to have worked with the finest of brushes. All traces of painting vanish; we are far removed from the exuberant brushstrokes of Frans Hals and the earthy energy of Brouwer. As if to challenge the impossible, Dou had a special liking for painting the very source of his light, the flame of a candle or a lantern. The color is almost transparent; the meticulous rendering of each surface—be it linen, glass, metal or a girl's face—is nearly flawless in its scrupulous reproduction of detail. In Dou the knack of mirroring nature came to smooth perfection; and, unlike many of his colleagues, he earned from his work great popularity and a comfortable existence. In the process, however, he sometimes became so preoccupied with matter that the spark of inspiration vanished from his painting.

In the next generation of Dutch genre artists, however, that spark was to become brighter than ever. Genre painting became less boisterous and more subtle, less mechanical and more subjective, until it well-nigh resembled still-life painting; and the genre painters proved once and for all that it is not the nobility or beauty of the subject that makes a good painting—only the way the artist sees and records it. In this respect the Dutch genre artists hewed a path all their own. At the end of that road we shall find Vermeer.

Celebrating Daily Life

With the rapid growth of a moneyed middle class in 17th Century Holland, something happened to art that had never happened before—a mass market for pictures sprang up. Under this impetus, the popular categories of still life and genre flourished. The best paintings —considered investments by the people who bought them—were sold by art dealers like Vermeer and his father. Others were vended at fairs and apparently even hawked by peddlers in the streets. Hardly a Dutch home was without a painting of some sort, and one amazed English visitor reported that "many times blacksmithes, cobblers, etts., will have some picture or other by their forge and in their stalle."

Reflecting the practical concerns of a practical people, Dutch art could at times be as gloomily moralistic as the still life shown here. But more often than not it hid its message, if any, under the lighthearted trappings of everyday life. A painting of a gorgeous banquet, executed with all the lush techniques at the artist's command, or a picture of a tipsy family, portrayed with broad good humor and a winking eye, had to amuse first, preach later—as though the sober moral were only the excuse for the subject, the antidote to the hangover. Out of this carefree attitude came an array of charming and witty paintings that delighted their owners and vividly show the 20th Century viewer what it was like to be Dutch and alive in the golden years of the 17th Century.

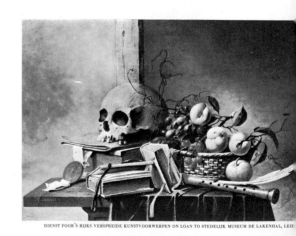

DIENST FOOR'S RIJKS VERSPREIDE KUNSTVOORWERPEN ON LOAN TO STEDELIJK MUSEUM DE LAKENHAL, LEID

Art with a moral, this still life, known as a *vanitas,* is of a type much admired by dour Calvinists. The deed, fruit and books stand for the possessions and earthly pleasures which the Dutch loved —but which, as the skull suggests, are rendered vain by death.

Harmen van Steenwijck: *Vanitas,* c. 1655. Detail, right

Willem Kalf: *Still Life*, 1659

Never has still-life painting been so popular as it was in the 17th Century, and the reason is easy to understand: the subject lent itself admirably to display in the home. What was at first a narrow category expanded rapidly into a broad one, producing subdivisions of its own that ranged from the allegorical *vanitas* of the preceding page through burgeoning flower studies to table and banquet pieces, of which the paintings by Willem Kalf *(above)* and Jan Davidsz. de Heem *(right)* are particularly rich examples. The Dutch even gave still life its poetic name, although their word *stilleven* originally meant simply "motionless model."

The challenge for still-life painters lay in making beautiful things look real. One of Kalf's hallmarks is his evocation of an object through accents —through the glimmer of light on the overturned glass in the painting above, for example. The English diarist Samuel Pepys found himself so entranced by such effects that he had to put his finger to some painted dew "to feel whether my eyes are deceived or no." But lest the soul be deceived as well, especially by lush renderings of food and drink, artists usually took care to include in their works sobering reminders of life's transience, like the gold pocket watch and fragile butterflies in De Heem's otherwise hedonistic painting.

Jan Davidsz. de Heem: *Still Life with Lobster*, c. 1650

Gerard Terborch: *A Company in an Interior*, c. 1654

Genre, like still life, found many enthusiastic supporters among a people who enjoyed seeing themselves, their daily amusements and their cozy homes depicted in paintings. Its practitioners were numerous, and they worked at various levels of Dutch society, with different audiences in mind. Gerard Terborch, represented here by two of his most intimate works, belonged to the upper class, and his paintings display an opulence that shows he intended them to hang in rich settings. And because he could apparently count on his patrons being wealthy connoisseurs, he lavished upon such appurtenances of wealth as a satin dress *(left)* all his talent for simulating the textures of things.

But despite his attention to such eye-catching detail, Terborch kept to the anecdotal mode of genre and in his own subtle way could be as racy a painter as any. The picture above used to be called *Parental Admonition* until someone, noticing the gold coin in the man's hand and the bedroom setting, thought better of the title. *Unwelcome News (opposite)* speaks with such forthrightness that there is no mistaking what it is about: posed against the background of a bed with his arm around a wench, a soldier gets word that he is being called back to duty.

A Company in an Interior, detail

Gerard Terborch: *Unwelcome News*, 1653

Dutch genre painters were quick to discover that art could be serious without having a serious subject, and many turned out pictures that were, and still are, funny. The one who enjoyed laughter most was Jan Steen, and he portrayed himself most appropriately in the painting at left, where he can be seen as the fat figure on the far side of the table, his head thrown back in a guffaw. The cause of all this merriment is Twelfth Night, a Dutch family celebration, and Steen has included, in addition to himself, his son, wearing a paper crown and taking a coronation drink, and his wife, who has just poured that drink and sprawls contentedly in her chair.

Apart from the delight the scene itself affords, there are esthetic pleasures here to be savored as well—the mastery with which Steen has composed the picture, the colors he has chosen to light up its surface, and the attention he has given to details as seemingly minor as eggshells cast casually on the checkered floor.

Jan Steen: *Twelfth Night*, 1668

87

Gabriel Metsu: *The Sick Child*, c. 1660

A hallmark of Dutch art is its humanity, and if a humorous note runs through much of genre, a sentimental tone is found there as well. It is present to varying degrees in these works by three other masters, most outspokenly in the painting by Nicolaes Maes *(below)* of an old woman at her prayers—the lugubrious aspect of which is offset by the cat that seems about to claw both tablecloth and meal onto the floor. After working out an almost geometrical interior for the painting at right, Pieter de Hoogh warms its cool space with a mother and child, so fondly portrayed as to suggest that these are not mere models but his wife and three-year-old son, dressed—according to the custom of the 17th Century—in skirts. Another mother-child relationship is explored tenderly in the painting by Gabriel Metsu *(opposite)*, who here shares many qualities with Vermeer but probes character far more deeply.

Pieter de Hoogh: *The Pantry*, c. 1658

Nicolaes Maes: *An Old Woman Saying Grace*, c. 1655

Adriaen van Ostade: *Peasants in an Inn*, 1654

Low life became a favorite subject for genre, possibly because of the satisfaction it gave those moneyed Dutchmen who felt themselves above such an existence. Adriaen van Ostade, the son of a weaver, was one of many artists who made the bumpkin their stock in trade; of his paintings on this subject hundreds still survive today.

Ostade offered his views of the peasants' life without social comment, portraying only their brief, hard-won moments of leisure, and never their hours of toil. But the very fidelity with which he depicted squat, burly types like those in these pictures going about their child-like games does much to reveal their pathetic side. The peasants, after all, were the people who had suffered most during the Eighty Years' War, and no matter how much their daily life may have seemed to improve with the advent of peace, it still was bounded by hardship, poverty, disease and death.

Adriaen van Ostade: *Peasants Dancing outside an Inn*, 1654

THE METROPOLITAN MUSEUM OF ART, THE MICHAEL FRIEDSAM COLLECTION, 1931

Adriaen Brouwer: *The Brawl*

BAYERISCHE STAATSGEMÄLDESAMMLUNGEN, MUNICH

Adriaen Brouwer: *Smell*

Adriaen Brouwer found the themes for his art in the very dregs of Dutch society, and fashioned from this unlikely material paintings so fine that they attracted collectors as perspicacious as Rembrandt and Rubens. Unlike Ostade, Brouwer seems not to be observing his subject so much as living it. If his biographers are to be believed, he was something of a wild fellow himself, having even spent time in prison.

Brouwer's fascination with low life sprang in part from the opportunity it gave him to paint people letting go—like the brawlers at top left or the pipe-drunk smokers below.

Although his paintings have something of a sketchy quality and are almost always small (the one reproduced opposite is actually only a little over five inches high) he was a meticulous craftsman. He selected his details carefully, allowing no unnecessary notes to intrude: his backgrounds are usually neutral, carrying the tones of dark, smoke-filled and dank rooms. He made his paintings come alive, as has been said, with "the totality of a swift gesture or of a tight network of gestures." And it is this impassioned quality that seems to have been a reflection of his own character and a trait that hastened his death at 32. A contemporary verse summed up his brief career:

He never despised what the world on
  him pressed:
He painted but slowly, could spend
  like the best,
And in smelly low taverns smoke his
  pipe with a zest.

Adriaen Brouwer: *Youth*

V

A Flowering
of Brilliance

This merry skating scene by
Hendrick Avercamp combines
the elements of traditional
indoor genre painting with
the notion of pure landscape
—an idea that was to flourish
in Holland. Winter scenes such
as this have been called "the
Dutch 17th Century landscape
painting *par excellence.*"

Hendrick Avercamp: *A Winter
Scene with Skaters near a Castle*

The Dutch Golden Age produced so many artists in such a short time
that it is hard to separate them into distinct generations. For example,
Frans Hals, Rembrandt and Jan Vermeer are often thought of as representing, respectively, the early, middle and late periods of the era; yet
their life-spans so overlapped that for more than a decade they were all
painting at the same time, and all three died within a nine-year period.

Nevertheless, a rough dividing line can be drawn between such painters as Hals, Avercamp and Terbrugghen, who pioneered the new styles of
painting, and those younger painters who grew up with artistic idioms
that were already established. These men, born generally after 1620,
were Vermeer's contemporaries and were the painters who carried Gold-
en Age art into its final brilliance. They were not necessarily greater
artists than their elders but they tended to paint with more sophistica-
tion, more smoothness, and their work represented a summing up of
the era's various artistic expressions.

This was particularly true of landscape painting, which reached a peak
in the work of Philips Koninck and Jacob van Ruisdael. (The latter should
not be confused with Salomon van Ruysdael, a lesser known artist
who was Jacob's uncle and teacher.) Except for one or two masterpieces by later painters—including a very special example by Meindert
Hobbema—no one had anything essential to add to landscape painting
after these two artists.

Koninck, born in 1619, lived in Amsterdam and made his mark in
the workaday world as the owner of a ferry service between his city and
Rotterdam. But his enduring achievement was the painting of some
70 portraits of the Dutch countryside, executed with such power that,
despite several centuries of neglect, he is today considered one of the
masters of his time.

It has been said that the most important contribution to landscape
painting made by Dutch painters was the panorama, and Koninck was
supreme in this expression. His pictures *(pages 110-111)* are filled with
patches of sunlight on vast, dark fields; his horizons stretch evenly across
the canvas, dividing earth and sky into almost equal parts. His vantage

point is well elevated so that obstructions such as hills or trees rarely rise high enough to break the line between the viewer and the misty horizon where the colors have become dim. The result is a sense of great space and serenity. The sky usually is filled with dramatic clouds, which make dynamic an otherwise tranquil scene.

Koninck's view of nature in these paintings, though entirely free from fussy detail, is essentially realistic. That is not to say it is completely true to life. Koninck made a selection of the features of the countryside before him and composed his picture with a feeling for esthetic effect. In this he moved away from the precise rendering of nature that characterized much of the work of the early landscapists.

Ruisdael carried this subjective trend further and applied it more widely. Not only in panoramas but also in forest scenes, seascapes and beach scenes, he manipulated reality in a subtle, almost imperceptible way to serve his artistic purpose. One of his most famous paintings, of the windmill near the little town of Wijk bij Duurstede *(pages 118-119)*, is an illustration of Ruisdael's genius for reshaping nature to create art. A similar mill stands now where the original did, and the scene is much as it was 300 years ago, but it makes a much less striking impression in reality than in the painting. Ruisdael's artistic construction—the contrasting of colors and of light and dark, as well as a clever use of verticals and diagonals—has made the simple mill monumental, almost threatening, and as romantic and imposing as a medieval castle.

Dutch landscape painting is often thought of as being an unemotional, uniformly tranquil record of placid country scenes. The work of Ruisdael reveals how inappropriate this notion can be. Many Ruisdael paintings are touched by a melancholy that echoes the gloomy musings of the early landscapist Hercules Seghers. Ruisdael's *Burst of Sunlight* is a good example. It has a grave, brooding quality and an air of drama. On a wide river valley, with a town lost in shadow in the background and a somber ruin on the left, a sudden flood of sunlight strikes an old brick bridge. A man on horseback, wrapped in a red cloak, has just crossed the bridge, and Ruisdael makes it clear that the rider has left behind the safety of the town and that a long road lies ahead of him in the gathering twilight. The mood is intensified by a vast sky—filled with towering clouds sculptured in sunlight and shadow—that occupies at least two thirds of the canvas.

The feeling of reality is so strong in Ruisdael's landscapes, even when he altered reality by his emotional and often somber vision, that it comes as a surprise to learn that he and his contemporary landscapists never actually painted outdoors. They all made sketches on the scene, but painted in the studio, relying on sketchbook and memory. Nevertheless, Ruisdael's knowledge of the things he painted was profound. Time and again he set out from Haarlem for the nearby village of Overveen close to the North Sea, climbed the dunes and spent hours absorbing the sights around him.

He had a poetic feeling for nature that was almost mystical, a sense of the power of nature that led him to reduce man in his paintings to the role of bit player. No Dutch landscapist ever completely eliminated man and his works from the scene—in the crowded countryside of Holland there were very few unpeopled vistas. So in Ruisdael's haunting *View of Haarlem (page 118)*, painted from the sand dunes of Overveen, workers are shown bleaching cloth in the fields, but they are subordinated to nature. It is the fields themselves that are important, and it is the trees and clouds and light, so lovingly observed by Ruisdael, that are dominant.

Ruisdael may stand out today as a pre-eminent artist, but in his own time he was just one of hundreds of landscapists who filled the market with their wares. One comprehensive study lists some 250 Dutch landscapists of the 17th Century, dozens of whom made important artistic contributions. The competition among them made earning a living very difficult for all painters except those lucky enough to be in the public eye at the time.

Whatever bad effects it may have had on the local market, this great flood of canvases helped to spread the influence of Dutch landscape painting beyond Holland's borders. Thousands of paintings of the Dutch countryside found their way into foreign collections, where they could be seen and admired by the 18th and 19th Century landscapists of France, England and Italy.

Two Dutch landscape artists who exerted a significant influence abroad—particularly in England—were Albert Cuyp and Meindert Hobbema. Cuyp, born about 1620, was a well-to-do gentleman farmer and magistrate in the town of Dordrecht; he did not depend on his painting for a livelihood and he was not particularly well known during his lifetime. But in the 18th Century the works of Cuyp became so popular in England that collectors there traveled to Holland to buy every canvas by him they could find. As a gentleman of the soil, Cuyp had a special skill in depicting animals and farmland *(pages 108-109)* that appealed particularly to the English gentry. Even today, most of the best of Cuyp's paintings are in England and he is not very well represented in his own country's museums.

Cuyp's work was not consistently good but the best was very good indeed. His landscapes, often populated by horses and cows, are bathed in sunlight, and everything is quieter, more evenly lit, than in the works of many of his contemporaries. His *Herdsman with Five Cows, by a River*, one of nine Cuyps in London's National Gallery, is filled with the soft light and tranquillity of the countryside just before sunset, when dusk descends and tempers light and contrasts. There is in this and other Cuyp masterpieces a glow that has earned him the title "The Dutch Claude" after the French landscapist Claude Lorrain, whose landscapes were also bathed in a golden vapor.

Meindert Hobbema was one of the last—perhaps *the* last—of the great landscapists of the Golden Age, and he was another great favorite with English art lovers of the 18th and 19th Centuries. Born in 1638, he was briefly a pupil of Ruisdael, but his rendering of nature was less moody than that of his master. He dealt with a more limited number of motifs, painting mostly forest scenes and water mills, and in these views he came closer to nature and watched it with more of an eye to detail than did his teacher. Hobbema was a masterly painter of trees; he painted hundreds of them, and with never failing subtlety recorded their myriad variations of color and form.

With one great exception, Hobbema painted his best work as a young man, during the 1660s. In 1668 he secured a well-paying city job in Amsterdam, and very few paintings dated after that have been found. But then, two decades later, in 1689, he painted the crowning achievement of his career: *The Avenue, Middelharnis (pages 116-117)*.

In this famous painting there is a delicate balance between space and matter that gives it lightness and grace; and yet there is great strength in the few thin, sky-reaching trees, in the sure composition that deftly opposes horizontal and vertical emphasis. Whatever the circumstances that produced this stroke of genius in Hobbema's middle age, it is unquestionably one of the finest landscapes of the century. Furthermore, no Dutch landscape paintings of great worth came after *Avenue;* it was the capstone to the Golden Age.

There were many other kinds of artists besides landscapists competing for the public's attention during the later years of this great era. Among the most prolific were the hundreds of painters still working in the various styles of genre initiated by the earlier generation. One of the most productive and well-known of these was Jan Steen, whose chronicling of feasts, drinking bouts and scenes of low life put him in an indirect line of succession from Adriaen Brouwer and Adriaen van Ostade. But Steen was also a master at painting children—he had many of his own whom he used as models—and he showed them with great tenderness and perception.

There is a strong anecdotal quality to much of Steen's work which accounted in part for his popularity in the 17th Century, but there is more to his art than simple storytelling. At his best, Steen was just as interested in the play of light and color around his subjects as he was in the story those subjects told. Despite his irreverent subject matter he was an extremely serious artist, and his wild inn scenes, at first sight so abandoned and haphazard, show the marks of painstaking study and care. (It is now generally agreed that some noticeably rough paintings attributed to him were either the work of his students or were done hastily by Steen for quick money.)

Steen, who married the daughter of landscapist Jan van Goyen, operated a brewery in Delft for a few years and he was almost certainly familiar with the work of Vermeer during that time. There is no clear evidence, however, that Steen and Vermeer influenced each other. In fact, except for his interest in light, Steen was very unlike Vermeer in his approach to painting. There was little of the contemplative in Steen; his view was essentially reportorial. He took a lively, personal interest in the activities of people around him and with great humor he showed them playing games, eating, drinking, celebrating holidays *(pages 86-87)*. His enormous output of paintings—about 800 of them altogether, including allegorical and religious themes—offers one of the finest records of 17th Century Dutch life.

Although Steen had little in common with Vermeer, other genre painters of the later generation produced works that were similar in

Gerard Terborch revealed his interest in costume at an early age; he was only eight when he began sketching the society friends of his father. But Gerard had not yet developed the genius for understatement that was to grace his mature works; here he displays a childish taste for extravagance.

many ways to the Delft master's. Four of the finest of these artists were Gerard Terborch, Gabriel Metsu, Nicolaes Maes and Pieter de Hoogh, whose work shared some important characteristics: they all painted in soft, luminous colors; they all specialized in interior scenes, well-illuminated and carefully composed with only a few figures; and their work, compared with that of Steen, was subdued and tranquil. Furthermore, they freely borrowed situations for their subject matter from one another and from other artists, as was the custom of the time. So great were the similarities between Vermeer and these gifted contemporaries that during the 18th and 19th Centuries many of his paintings were passed off as theirs by shrewd art dealers who could get more for their work than for that of the forgotten Vermeer.

Gerard Terborch was fortunate enough to have been appreciated in his own day as well as by later generations. In two respects he was an exception in the art world of his time: he was a worldly man and, through his marriage, he was well off. (He was also the only important painter to hail from the East Netherlands province of Overijssel.) He dressed elegantly and traveled a good deal; in his formative years he had worked in London and Rome and is said by some authorities to have traveled to Spain after the peace treaty of 1648 and to have painted a portrait of King Philip IV.

As a young man Terborch had a penchant for portraying military men off duty—usually drinking or visiting the ladies; it was a favorite subject of the time, and one which Vermeer also painted early in his career. Terborch approached such earthy subject matter without the slightest touch of lewdness or innuendo—he was much too sophisticated for that. His genre was of a subtle sort: his persons, rarely more than three, pose in vaguely delineated space; his colors are subdued, his forms most carefully fashioned. In his later, and perhaps most admired paintings, he turned from his soldiers to concentrate on women, richly dressed in satins and glowing silks, elegantly arranged in evenly-lit interiors against dark backgrounds *(pages 84-85)*.

Terborch also produced one of the finest historical paintings of the Dutch 17th Century, the *Treaty of Münster,* showing the Spanish and Dutch delegates at the treaty-signing in 1648 that ratified the Netherlands' independence. The contemporary historical scene is a rarity in Dutch painting; few Dutch artists witnessed the great events of history, and they were not interested in painting what they could not see. But Terborch, more traveled than most, was in Münster during the negotiations. His painting, comprising more than 50 portraits on a panel measuring only 18 by 23 inches, is a vivid re-creation of a dramatic moment.

Gabriel Metsu was a close friend of Jan Steen's, and his art echoes some of Steen's conviviality, but his work generally is closer to Vermeer's in spirit. For instance, in his well-known genre piece, *The Letter,* Metsu shows an unmistakable debt to Vermeer both in his subject and in its execution. It is a painting of superb craftsmanship, showing the lady of the house in a yellow jacket bordered with ermine. On her pink skirt rests a red cushion and she is reading a letter; a maid, dressed in brown and blue, holds an envelope and is looking at a seascape hanging on the wall. The lady, the maid, the letter, some of the colors, even a seascape, are also to be found in Vermeer's *Love Letter (page 158)*.

But there is an important difference between Metsu and his colleagues and Vermeer. Vermeer has endowed the familiar scenes in his painting with an aloof, mysterious stillness that isolates the figures from the viewer and produces a suspended, timeless effect. Metsu, on the other hand, shows his little scene as though it were enacted for the painter and set down by him on canvas almost in a photographic manner: nothing is left out and nothing added. We visualize Metsu arranging his models, putting down a slipper, pushing a chair in place. He painted his figures *(page 88)* with warmth and understanding and makes the viewer feel part of the situation and the moment, but there is none of the spiritual distance from the subjects, the cool reserve that lifts Vermeer's work from the realm of the everyday.

Nicolaes Maes, another genre painter with a link to Vermeer, was also a painter of domestic scenes. He was a pupil of Rembrandt's, but he did not share his teacher's flamboyant personality or dramatic style. Maes was a quiet, gentle man, and his paintings deal with gentle subjects: a child rocking a cradle, a subdued, somewhat sad young girl sewing in a corner, a lonely old woman saying grace over her supper, which consists of one kipper on a tin plate *(page 89)*.

Some observers feel that the influence of Maes can be seen in the strong coloring and composition of Vermeer's *Girl Asleep*. Unlike Vermeer, Maes sometimes is overly sentimental, but he tells his little stories so unashamedly and with such fine craftsmanship that some of his work rates with the finest genre painting of the century.

The genre master who came closest to matching the perfection of Vermeer was Pieter de Hoogh. De Hoogh was only three years older than Vermeer and he lived in Delft for about seven years. He was certainly familiar with the work of Vermeer and it is very likely that they influenced each other. After De Hoogh moved to Amsterdam in 1662 he concentrated on elaborate and romantic portrayals of society, and the quality of his work greatly diminished. But while in Delft, painting the simple domestic scenes that were the chief subject of that city's painters, his artistry was superb.

De Hoogh had worked as a footman, which may account for the sense of pride in a well-kept house that is evident in his paintings. They usually show, with fine perspective, several rooms, one beyond the other; sunlight is everywhere and the rooms are filled with clean airiness and the sense of well-being that was a hallmark of the Dutch middle-class home *(pages 89, 130)*.

Some of De Hoogh's paintings are outdoor views of courtyards and streets, and in these the fall of noon sunlight, modulated by subtle shadows and color variations, is expressed with almost palpable realism. It was in this use of light, particularly, that De Hoogh most often reminds the viewer of Vermeer and comes nearest to being his peer.

Almost as popular as landscapes and genre paintings in the art stalls of the market place were paintings of still life. This specialty, which 17th Century Dutch artists raised to the status of a major art category, had long been admired by the Dutch public: displays of food had been included in some religious works and portraits in the 15th and 16th Centuries. Now inanimate objects were portrayed for their own sake. At first, such paintings were named after their subjects: a flower piece or a fruit piece; a composition showing a kipper and a glass of beer or some other arrangement of simple foods was called a breakfast picture; if the display was more lavish, it became a banquet picture. Not until the middle of the century did the category acquire the name *stilleven*— still life.

Though it started in the kitchen, still-life painting soon branched out to include the whole catalogue of decorative and useful items with which Dutch burghers surrounded themselves: silver tankards, half-filled wineglasses, tobacco pipes, musical instruments, parchment and globes, along with the usual fruits, vegetables and game. As the century wore on, still lifes reflected the increasing degree of middle-class luxury: by the late 1660s simple white tablecloths had given way to ornate Persian rugs and the china was often fine Ming. Such glorification of the Good Life matched the mood of the prosperous art buyer. The paintings obviously fit nicely on the wall over his dining table, and the artists who made them were assured of a steady demand.

At first these specialists often included an overt message in their work, as did the masters of genre. A popular theme of their paintings was the vanity of all earthly affairs, and the works were thus known as *vanitas* still lifes. They always included some objects that spoke of the impermanence of life—a skull or other bones, an hourglass, some flowers, a snuffed-out candle. There were countless other symbols, each with its special meaning; the sea-shell, a collector's item, represented wealth; musical instruments symbolized the pleasures of the senses; the Japanese sword was an emblem of military power. Some artists even painted still-life motifs for the enjoyment of clever observers who were supposed to guess the appropriate symbolism.

One place where the tradition of vanitas painting was strong was Leiden, possibly because the university there made that town a center of theological studies. It has been suggested that the vanitas painting played a role in Holland parallel to that of the crucifixes and religious paintings in Catholic countries—that it was a Protestant way of reminding the onlooker of the transience of human joys and earthly triumphs.

This symbolic emphasis diminished gradually as artists became more interested in the painting of a picture than in its message. For example, one prominent vanitas painter was Jan de Heem, who spent some years in Leiden; later he shifted his attention to flower and fruit pieces *(page 83)*. In these he could pay less attention to allegory and concentrate on the purely artistic effects of his subjects—on their color, texture and form. (The flower piece was highly popular in Holland and was long considered an essential part of the artist's training and a proof of his ability.)

Another artist who dealt surpassingly well with all aspects of still life was Willem Kalf, whose best years coincided with the prime of Dutch still-life painting—from 1640 to about 1670. Kalf was a marvelous craftsman, who could record with astonishing skill the fall of light

These careful little studies of a field mouse by Jacques de Gheyn reflect the growing interest of 17th Century Dutch artists in representing the natural world without religious or mythological overtones. De Gheyn, a master of still-life painting, and others received encouragement from scientists who sought accurate illustrations for their biological texts.

through colored crystal and wineglasses, or paint with sensuous precision the spiral curl of a lemon peel *(page 82)*.

But eventually Kalf and the other masters of still life, while continuing to cater profitably to the taste of their buyers, went far beyond the mere description of their subjects. They not only reflected the day's opulent taste in material objects but they also delighted in building pure patterns of color and light. In the hands of specialists like De Heem and Willem van Aelst of Delft, the composition of a flower piece became as important as the color range; the fall of light and shade was felt to be as interesting as the bouquet of brilliant hues.

In this sense still-life painting—and particularly the work of Kalf— is related to the painting of Vermeer. Vermeer is not known to have executed any pure still lifes, but it has often been noted that he captured the essence of the best of this specialty: like still-life painting, the works of the Master of Delft transcend the limitations of their ordinary subjects to embody a more universal vision of form and beauty.

Another artistic specialty of the time that had an effect on Vermeer was architectural painting *(pages 68-69)*. In the earlier generation of painters, a master of this form was Pieter Saenredam, who was the first to abandon the fanciful treatment that had dominated earlier architectural painting. With an unerring control of perspective, and with geometric precision, he painted the lines and curves of the arches, vaults and columns of dozens of church interiors. Known as the "first portraitist of architecture," Saenredam was meticulously faithful to reality. If, in his drawing of a building, Saenredam changed a line or a detail from the actuality, he made a careful note to that effect so that the viewer would not be misled.

Emanuel de Witte, another architectural painter, born in 1617, took a different approach. His imposing interiors, with their vaulted ceilings and vast open spaces, were not necessarily drawn from reality, but often came from his imagination. Still, his structures were so convincingly solid that they always conveyed an unshakable *impression* of reality. One of the ways he did this was by capturing to perfection the effect of sunlight on the surfaces, both inside and outside, of the buildings he painted; he learned to manipulate light and shadow to suggest the texture and feeling of brick and stone as they had never been shown before. This achievement was not lost on De Witte's contemporaries in Delft, where he worked for about 10 years. The mastery of Vermeer, De Hoogh and other Delft masters in rendering the walls, streets and courtyards of their city owes a great deal to De Witte.

Among all Vermeer's contemporaries, the artist who had the most effect on him was Carel Fabritius, the brilliant young painter who died in the Delft gunpowder explosion of 1654. Even though there is not sufficient evidence to prove that Fabritius was actually Vermeer's teacher, there is in the paintings of the two men unmistakable evidence that the younger artist admired and learned from the other's work. (When Vermeer died he owned two or three Fabritius paintings.)

Fabritius' output was very small, and while it includes some portraits and a few genre paintings his place in Dutch art is not easy to assess.

His work is often spoken of as forming a spiritual bridge between Rembrandt and Vermeer. Fabritius studied under Rembrandt in Amsterdam before moving to Delft; his early work, such as the so-called *Self-Portrait* (it is by no means certain that the portrait is of the artist) is Rembrandtesque in its warm coloring and dramatic play of light and shadow. But his later work, painted after he moved to Delft, foreshadows much of the cool harmony of color and compact composition that mark the art of Vermeer.

Two Fabritius paintings in particular invite comparison with Vermeer. His *View in Delft*, while quite different from Vermeer's great *View of Delft*, shares with that picture a sensitive mastery of perspective and the effects of warm sunlight on the town's red brick buildings. (The Fabritius work has a curious composition, involving the exaggeration of several curves and angles, that has led some experts to speculate that it was designed for a viewing-box. This instrument was a kind of peep show that provided a stereoscopic effect—a popular device of the day that reflected the unusual interest of the Dutch in optics and perspective.)

The Sentinel (page 71), one of Fabritius' last pictures, also hints strongly of Vermeer. The subject, a soldier supposedly on watch, but dozing with his firearm laid carelessly across his knees, is remote from any that Vermeer painted. But the mood it creates is very close to Vermeer. The picture, in spite of its explicit subject, does not merely tell a prosy anecdote; it is painted with a cool detachment that gives the effect of poetry whose appeal lies not in its immediate story line but in its timeless balance of tones and forms.

But it is Fabritius' exquisite little *Goldfinch (page 70)*, painted in the year of his death, that leads most directly to the genius of Vermeer. The picture, depicting a small bird chained to a seed chest, displays several effects and techniques that are characteristic of Vermeer: the dark figure of the bird is shaded in extraordinarily effective relief against a light-colored wall; the shadows and light areas delicately reflect and absorb the colors around them; the shapes of the bird and its perch give an almost three-dimensional effect of depth and substance. Here again Fabritius, like Vermeer, is describing reality accurately, but in a medium that is poetic, not photographic. Furthermore, graceful as it is, the picture has a strength, a compactness, a controlled mastery of space that is to be found elsewhere only in the work of Vermeer.

When Fabritius died, the Golden Age was in full bloom. The landscapists, genre artists, still-life specialists and architectural painters of the younger generation were at the height of their powers, turning out a profusion of superb paintings. Vermeer, one of the last of the generation, would soon add his brilliant luster to their achievement. And then suddenly, within two decades of Fabritius' death, the bloom faded. With a few exceptions there was no one left after Vermeer, no other generation to carry on.

The glorious era of Dutch painting that had begun with Frans Hals early in the century was barely 50 years old when Vermeer and his contemporaries carried it to its brightest flowering. When they were gone, the Golden Age was over.

A Love
for the Land

In the years following 1600, after nearly half a century of bone-wearying wars, a measure of peace finally came to Holland. Together with their countrymen, Dutch painters began to look with a fierce new pride, almost religious in intensity, at the bountiful land for which they and their fathers had fought. Thus the great era of Dutch landscape painting was born.

Landscape elements had always been present in Dutch art, but usually only as a backdrop or stage setting; now the land was being painted for its own beauty. This was no task for amateur painters: in a land where there are no Niagaras or Alps, where everything is on a familiar, human scale, where much of the land is even man-made, it required exceptional sensitivity and skill to draw and paint landscapes as breathtaking as the etching shown opposite. The best Dutch painters discovered a wide range of subject matter: Meindert Hobbema became famous for his woodsy scenes, Willem van de Velde the Younger for his seascapes, Philips Koninck for his panoramic views. Jacob van Ruisdael, perhaps the greatest painter of all, was adept at all forms of landscapes. Despite their achievements, few of these artists became wealthy: Koninck owned a ferry service; Hobbema collected taxes on wine, and Jan van Goyen speculated unluckily in the tulip market. There can be no doubt, though, that each of them was satisfied, proud of his art, and proud of his peaceful land.

This etching by Vermeer's greatest contemporary is a perfect landscape: the earth stirs with human activity of many sorts, the land itself is full of contrasts, and the brightening sky is alive with drama.

Rembrandt van Rijn: *The Three Trees*, 1643

106

Hendrick Goltzius: *Study of a Tree*

Claes Jansz. Visscher: *The Bridge*

In Holland, as elsewhere, the art of black and white often anticipated subsequent discoveries in painting. This was especially true in the opening years of the 17th Century, when artists were just beginning to explore and record the myriad subject possibilities of the Dutch countryside. Not only could the etcher or engraver in black and white turn out more work than the painter, but his art could also be reproduced by the hundreds or thousands on loose sheets or bound into books—an important consideration at that time, when a large public was eager for art but could not afford to purchase expensive paintings.

But the importance of these graphic artists goes far beyond mere productivity. For one thing, through their interest in a truthful depiction of nature they helped to free landscape painting from its traditional limitation as merely a setting for allegorical, mythological or Biblical subjects. Goltzius' *Study of a Tree (left)*, for instance, is simply that—branch by branch and leaf by leaf. Also, in making their work available to a wide audience the etchers and engravers helped to create a taste for landscape. As Claes Jansz. Visscher, who drew the simple canal scene above, wrote on the title page of a series of his prints, "Here you may have a quick look at pleasant places, you art lovers who have no time to travel far."

107

Aelbert Cuyp: *Landscape with Trees*

Despite his interest in the outdoors, the Dutch landscape painter rarely painted there. His usual practice was to make sketches of scenes that caught his eye; then, returning to his studio, he would begin to paint, using his drawings for reference. And since he might use as many as a dozen drawings from different locations in a single painting, the final scene was often almost entirely the product of his imagination.

One of the most brilliant draftsman-painters was Aelbert Cuyp, three of whose drawings are shown here. Selecting such unprepossessing scenes as a boat bobbing at anchor, cows along a riverbank and gnarled trees beside a country road, Cuyp has managed to convey in black and white an impression of what the Dutch countryside was really like—no forested wilderness but a tended land of poetic charm and simplicity.

Aelbert Cuyp: *Fishing Boat*

Aelbert Cuyp: *Landscape with River and Cows*

Philips Koninck: *View over a Flat Landscape with a River*, 1664

Willem van de Velde the Younger: *Ships Saluting in a Calm*, date unknown

Holland is more intimately linked with the sea than almost any nation on the earth. It is not surprising, therefore, that a number of Dutch artists devoted their careers to seascapes. Willem van de Velde the Younger was particularly enchanted by the sea; he sailed with the navy during the war and kept a stirring record of the conflict in vigorous drawings like the one above.

While Dutch artists had little difficulty in finding dramatic subjects at sea, the land, with its monotonous flatness, posed a more awkward problem. Their solution was to meet the problem directly and to portray the country in all its breadth. They invented the panorama—a broad view of earth and sky constructed on a sweeping scale—an elementary idea to the 20th Century viewer, but a revolutionary concept to the audience of Vermeer's time. Having found an avenue of attack, Dutch artists were still faced with the necessity of varying their compositions so that the ground was broken up into interesting shapes and the sky did not overbalance the land. Some artists chose an elevated viewpoint, dividing their canvases almost evenly between earth and sky; others chose the ground-level view and found ways to add visual interest to their scenes.

Philips Koninck, a pupil of Rembrandt, became especially noted for his panoramas, one of which is shown at left. Viewing the land from a height —perhaps a windmill or a hillock—Koninck uses a meandering river as a bold diagonal running from lower right to upper left. He also introduces a wooded ravine at lower left, to balance the composition. Two rounded dunes at center hold the viewer's eye momentarily before the panorama sweeps mistily into the background. It was with geometric devices like these that Koninck and the other great Dutch landscape artists added a dynamic quality to pictures of their pleasant country.

Esajas van de Velde: *The Ferry Boat*, 1622

Although it is impossible to single out one artist as the father of Dutch landscape painting, the likeliest candidate is Esajas van de Velde, whose career marks the transition from drawing to painting. Van de Velde was a fine draftsman who began to work in color at an early stage. Most of his paintings are tied to the traditions of genre, in which people and their activities predominate. In the work shown here, attention is focused on the crowded ferry, the bankside strollers and the bustling boatyard. Van de Velde's reliance on genre elements may have been due to the conservative tastes of his patrons, who insisted upon people in their art. To satisfy himself, however, he attempted difficult compositions. Here, he has composed three elements—sky, earth and water—in a harmonious relationship; the gently curving flow of water creates a convincing sense of depth, the tall, open-leafed trees break the flat sky, and the high steeple and windmill interrupt the horizon line, anchoring the composition in the background.

The Ferry Boat, deta

Jan van Goyen carried forward the concept of the panoramic view: the human figure almost disappears in his paintings, which are pure landscapes. Perhaps his greatest contribution was the use of zigzagging diagonals; in the work above they proceed from both sides and lead the eye farther and farther back. Van Goyen also used

Jan van Goyen: *The Beacon*, 1637

color to achieve a sense of depth; dark tones in the foreground become progressively lighter until land meets sky. And although his works were often monochromatic, the muted hues create an extraordinary effect of real weather, along with the conviction that the artist has pictured the precise moment just before a rainfall.

Jacob van Ruisdael: *View of Haarlem*, c. 1670

Jacob van Ruisdael was the supreme genius of the Dutch landscapists, the only one who fully mastered every type of landscape painting from the broad panorama to the most delicate, intimate view. Every time he touched his brush to canvas he seems to have created a masterwork.

The subject that Ruisdael most often painted was his beloved home town, Haarlem, which he always portrayed in the full bloom and warmth of midsummer. The painting above, showing a neatly tended field with linen bleaching in the hot sun in the foreground, is unusual in 17th Century Dutch outdoor art because of its vertical composition; most landscapes, including Ruisdael's own, were composed horizontally. Here, however, the artist has let the sky dominate—it occupies more than two thirds of the canvas.

Indeed, if any one aspect of Ruisdael's work can be singled out over others, it is his treatment of the sky. Perhaps, finding little of nature's wildness left in the man-ordered territory at his feet, he sought the drama overhead. In any case, Ruisdael managed in paintings like the one at right—in which clouds and sky also predominate—to project his feeling for nature's grandeur with the greatest skill. This quality, which set him above his fellow painters, later led the great 19th Century English landscapists John Constable and J.M.W. Turner to rediscover Ruisdael, to study his techniques, and, indeed, to make him the model for some of their own work.

Jacob van Ruisdael: *The Mill at Wijk bij Duurstede*, c. 1670

VI

Discovering the "Sphinx of Delft"

To the people of Delft who knew Vermeer it must have seemed that his life ended in sad failure. His last few years were filled with hardship and uncertainty; and when he died in 1675, leaving a wife and eight minor children, he was practically penniless.

As a matter of fact, things were bad for everyone in Holland at the time. In 1672 Louis XIV of France, who resented the Dutch for their prosperity and coveted their Rhine River ports on the North Sea, sent his armies into the Dutch Republic; within a few months they had swept over most of the country. The invasion came at a time when Dutch initiative and energy had begun to lag, and almost immediately the once-vigorous economy went into a sharp decline that affected every phase of the country's life. The government, finding itself in urgent need of funds, imposed first a sales tax, then a poll tax, then a land tax; finally the Dutch citizens had to make a compulsory loan to their hard-pressed government. Trade suffered and prosperity withered. Shaken by the troubled times, the art market collapsed.

It was at about this time that Vermeer was asked to give his opinion of the value of some paintings sold by a Dutch art dealer to the Elector of Brandenburg. After Vermeer's judgment against him, the dealer bitterly complained about the bad state of his business "since the value of all things and especially of paintings and such rarities has come to fall and decline in price in these calamitous times." He might have been speaking for the whole art world of the Netherlands.

For Vermeer, both artist and dealer, the situation apparently was doubly hard. Various documents indicate that by the time of the invasion, income from the dealership that was his livelihood had diminished almost to nothing; in testimony given after his death, Vermeer's widow Catharina explained that during his last years Vermeer had "been compelled to get rid of the art, which he had bought and in which he dealt, to his great disadvantage."

No one knows for certain whether these reverses were responsible or not, but it was at this time, 1672, that Vermeer moved from his house Mechelen on the market square to a smaller house on a street called

Enclosed within her world, a girl making lace bends to her task with a concentration that must reflect Vermeer's own attitude toward work. By foreshortening and blurring the foreground objects, he gave this jewel-like canvas (reproduced here in its actual size) a striking sense of intimacy.

The Lacemaker

Oude Langendijk several blocks away. The effect on his painting must have been shattering. Not only had he always lived in Mechelen, but apparently all his painting had been done in a few of its rooms. After leaving Mechelen he probably painted at most one or two pictures, and possibly none at all.

The French armies were driven out of the Republic in 1673 (once again the Dutch had defended their land by opening the dikes); but in the summer of 1675 Louis XIV threatened again, and the citizens of Delft were called out to build a defensive rampart around the town. It is not known whether Vermeer was healthy enough to join in the civic effort (which, it turned out, was unnecessary: the French never reached Delft) but it seems unlikely for, on December 15, the following entry was inscribed in the burial register of the Old Church: "Jan Vermeer, artist of the Oude Langendijk, [buried] in the Church." In the margin was a note: "Eight minors."

Almost immediately a struggle began between Vermeer's widow and his creditors—who found very little to lay their hands on except several dozen paintings. Some of these were by other artists, but 29 were by Vermeer himself, paintings for which there evidently had been no buyers during his lifetime.

Catharina seems to have tried desperately to keep her husband's works. In January 1676 she appeared before a notary with a baker, one Hendrik van Buyten, who was holding two paintings by Vermeer as collateral against a bread bill of more than 600 guilders. Van Buyten agreed to give back the paintings if the debt were paid off with a down payment followed by 50-guilder annual installments.

That the baker was willing to let the Vermeers run up such a huge debt in the first place is probably explained by the fact that Vermeer's mother-in-law was a woman of property who could ultimately be held responsible. She had, in fact, been able to lend Vermeer 1,000 guilders several months before he died; this was another debt Catharina had to pay off. She did so by signing over to her mother Vermeer's *An Artist in His Studio (pages 164-167)*, and, no doubt more important at that time, half the income from some land she owned near Rotterdam.

But there was not enough money to make ends meet. In April 1676, Catharina declared herself bankrupt, inventory was made of everything left in the house and a receiver of the estate was appointed. He was Anton van Leeuwenhoek, scientist and pioneer in the use of the microscope, who four years later would become a fellow of the Royal Society of London because of his observations of the microscopic world. In 1676, however, he made his living as a clerk to the town bailiff of Delft, and it was in this capacity that he became involved in the Vermeers' affairs. Many writers have seen a link between Vermeer, the master of light, and Leeuwenhoek, a master of optical science, but there is no proof of a friendship between them—indeed, Leeuwenhoek's behavior as executor appears to have been bureaucratic and unsympathetic.

At the sale of the bankrupt estate, a woman merchant named Jannetje Stevens managed to have 26 paintings by Vermeer seized and held as security against a family debt of 500 guilders "for groceries supplied."

Among the few documents that reveal any of Vermeer's life statistics is this note from the Delft public records which states that the aldermen of the city designate the great microscopist Anton Leeuwenhoek as receiver in the bankruptcy case of Catharina Bolnes, Vermeer's widow. It is dated September 30, 1676, a year after the artist's death. Ironically, both men's names appear on another page in the Delft ledger: the one recording their births in 1632.

Catharina protested the seizure and the size of the debt; it was agreed that if she paid 342 guilders immediately the pictures would be returned. But the records, so complete in some respects, fail in this case to tell whether Catharina ever saw the paintings again.

The following spring another Vermeer painting was threatened. Leeuwenhoek announced the bankruptcy sale of *An Artist in His Studio,* presumably on the ground that he could not recognize as legal the transfer of the painting within the family. Catharina's mother objected vigorously, but Leeuwenhoek refused to stop the proceedings. Once again the records fail to finish the story; they do not state whether the picture was actually sold.

Little more is known about the struggles of Catharina Vermeer to keep her family and her husband's work intact. Her situation obviously worried her mother, who willed her an annuity of 486 guilders to be paid monthly, or quarterly, as her daughter "perhaps does not receive sufficient victuals." Catharina died in 1687, and there were 12 pallbearers at her funeral, a mark of respect that suggests she was not a pauper. During the years since her husband's death three more of their children evidently had attained their majority, for the burial register records that she left five minors. That is about all the information we have about the family.

T he fate of the paintings is better known—though here, too, the record is sadly incomplete. Nine years after Catharina's death, 21 paintings by Vermeer were listed in the catalogue of an auction in Amsterdam that put up for sale 134 works by various artists. The Vermeer works may well have belonged to a private collector in Delft who had accumulated them as an investment. The average asking price for the 21 Vermeers was about 70 guilders—approximately $280—and most of the entries were enhanced by some encouraging words to prospective buyers such as "very beautiful," "very good" or "very artistically and powerfully painted."

That was the last time so many Vermeer paintings were ever gathered in one place. But to art historians the Amsterdam auction's chief importance lies in the catalogue descriptions of the 21 paintings—they comprise one of the few solid historical foundations critics have for determining what are genuine Vermeer paintings and what are not. Some of the descriptions are too vague to be of much use, and some of the paintings have vanished. But about 16 of those 21 have been identified today with considerable certainty. Had it not been for the auction, there might have been no record of the paintings at all, because that auction marked the last time for nearly 200 years that Vermeer's work received any but the most cursory public attention.

The history of a few of the paintings can be traced through those dark years—they usually changed hands as the work of Metsu, De Hoogh or Terborch, and often for paltry sums. Isolated voices spoke out occasionally in praise of Vermeer: Sir Joshua Reynolds mentioned the *Maidservant Pouring Milk* as one of the paintings he liked best during a trip to Holland in 1781; the French 19th Century authors and art critics Edmond and Jules de Goncourt wrote favorably in their diary of the same work, calling Vermeer a "devilishly original master." Otherwise, Vermeer suffered almost total eclipse during the 18th and most of the 19th Centuries, and even the lengthy scholarly volumes about the painters of the Golden Age that appeared during this time in Holland gave his art no space.

Then in 1866 Vermeer suddenly began to receive his due. The man responsible was an extraordinary French aristocrat, journalist, photographer and revolutionary named Etienne Joseph Théophile Thoré, who used the pen name William Bürger (German for "citizen"). Thoré-Bürger, as he is usually known now, had a particular interest in art, and during a visit to Holland in 1842 he had been profoundly impressed by a painting called *View of Delft* attributed to "Jan van der Meer of Delft." It hung in a gallery in The Hague, amidst dozens of other 17th Century paintings. "Aha," wrote Thoré-Bürger, "here is one we do not know in France and he very much deserves to be known."

Thoré-Bürger devoted a good deal of his life thereafter to the cause of making Vermeer well known. Exiled from France by Louis Napoleon in 1849 for his revolutionary activities, Thoré-Bürger spent much of his 10-year exile haunting the museums of England, Holland, Germany and Belgium in search of more works by Vermeer—whom he called "The Sphinx." Each painting he located intensified his admiration for Vermeer, and whenever possible he bought it or induced a friend to do so. He did not have the means himself to start a real collection, since his property had been confiscated at the time of his exile, but at one time or another he owned at least five Vermeers and many more passed through his hands.

With his knowledge of photography, Thoré-Bürger pioneered the use of photographs of the works of a master as an aid to documentation; he also corresponded with critics and curators who might help him in his search; and he applied his own judgment and energy. Altogether, his zealous detective work turned up more than 70 paintings he described as Vermeers, at least 50 of which he had seen himself. Another century of research has proved many of these to be of different origin, and has uncovered some Vermeers Thoré-Bürger did not find. But of the small total of undoubted Vermeers in existence today, some two thirds were identified by Thoré-Bürger.

Thoré-Bürger presented his opinions and findings about Vermeer in a series of articles and then in a little book in 1866. These eloquently communicated the author's enthusiasm to an art world that was just beginning to turn away from the traditional and to develop new ideas about esthetics—a world that was consequently prepared, at least in part, to judge Vermeer on his own terms.

Suddenly people began to take notice. Art dealers who had been selling Vermeers as Terborchs or De Hooghs now did a complete turnabout and started selling as Vermeers paintings that were not. Prices jumped; museums came to prize their Vermeers so much that transactions involving them came virtually to a standstill. As this is written, no generally accepted Vermeer has come up for auction for 50 years, and only four are privately owned. One of them, *Head of a Young Woman,* was acquired in 1955 for the collection of Mr. and Mrs. Charles Wrightsman. The reported price was $350,000.

Although there is little argument today about the value of Vermeer's art, there is still considerable debate about both the authenticity and the dates of certain of the works attributed to him. The questions of chronology and attribution are particularly troublesome in connection with Vermeer's first works, generally thought to be *Christ in the House of Mary and Martha (page 168)* and *Diana and Her Companions.* These are usually given the dates 1654 and 1655. Neither painting was in the catalogue of the 1696 auction. When the *Diana* came to light in 1876 it bore the signature of Nicholaes Maes; later, when it was cleaned, the canvas revealed an older signature, J. vMeer. A Vermeer signature was discovered on the *Christ* in 1901. Now *Diana* and the *Christ* are accepted as genuine Vermeers by most critics.

But a few disagree. The dissenting opinions are based on the differences between these two works and the rest of Vermeer's paintings—differences that are admittedly obvious at the most cursory glance. The Dutch critic P.T.A. Swillens pointed out some of the paintings' un-Vermeerian aspects: the religious and allegorical subjects; the dramatic, Caravaggesque treatment of light and contrast; the vague indication of the interior in the *Christ.* Swillens suggested that the *Christ* was done by a little-known but recognized painter named Jan van der Meer of Utrecht and raised the possibility that the *Diana* might even have been painted by Vermeer's father.

On the other hand, the uncharacteristic elements of these two paintings may be explained if they are accepted as being works of Vermeer's youth, before he arrived at the unique style of his mature years. Furthermore, there is much in the brilliant coloring in the two paintings that foreshadows Vermeer's later mastery of color; and in the *Diana,* the young girls' faces have tender, dreamy expressions that are very much in the manner of Vermeer. On the whole it seems most reasonable to agree with those art critics who judge the *Christ* and *Diana* to be the very earliest of Vermeer's known work.

It has been suggested that although with these pictures Vermeer proved his proficiency in the Italianate style of the Utrecht School, he decided he could not compete with its more established masters and so took another approach. Perhaps, on the other hand, he painted these first pictures just to prove he could do it, almost as an act of bravado, before he moved away from the art of the market place and assumed the quiet, personal style that marked his greatest works.

In what was probably his next painting, *The Procuress (page 65),* Vermeer came much closer to his mature style, but there are still strong echoes of his contemporaries' art. *The Procuress* is just as worldly a portrayal of the familiar genre scene as those by Baburen or Terbrugghen. It was painted with more of a flourish, and with its explicit story line was more appealing to the art buyer of the day, than most of Vermeer's later works. And yet the face of the girl in yellow has the inner radiance of all Vermeer's young women; with minor modifications it was to appear again and again in Vermeer's paintings.

It seems reasonable to believe that the model for the girl in *The Procuress*—and for the similar-looking women in many of the pictures that followed—was Vermeer's wife Catharina. Vermeer was so poor and worked so slowly that it is most unlikely he could afford a professional model. Furthermore, the face of the young woman was portrayed with a mixture of cool admiration, love and sensuality that a man could feel only for a woman he knew intimately.

Vermeer has often been completely misunderstood on the subject of women. Hasty observers have come away from a perusal of his paintings with the impression that the women in them were depicted by an artist as cold and realistic as the Dutch spice merchants and ship owners around him. But longer study shows that Vermeer, far from being cold, viewed women with tender admiration, almost with adoration; as one authority has written, his theme is "the sacredness of the woman who makes a happy and well-ordered home."

This treatment of woman is a key to Vermeer's art. During his major period he abandoned most extraneous subjects and confined himself almost entirely to the image of the young woman. There are exceptions—principally the *View of Delft* and the *Street in Delft,* both of which exemplify his finest work. And there is a brief final period when Vermeer's paintings became more complex and in some cases allegorical. But for the decade following 1658, when he did most of his best work, he concentrated on young women, alone or in various domestic situations.

There is, of course, more to Vermeer's paintings than the simple depiction of women. Again and again art scholars have mentioned the pearl as a perfect symbol for his work, not only because of the radiance of the young girls in his paintings or because so many of them wear pearl earrings or other pearl jewelry. The paintings themselves suggest pearls. Each of them is a perfect world, closed within itself, secret, softly lit, full of luster. In the 20th Century a Dutch painter and critic, Jan Veth, remarked that the substance of Vermeer's paint seems as if it were made of crushed pearls melted together.

It is possible upon examination of Vermeer's works to find some clues to how he achieved this almost magical effect. The most significant factor is his mastery of light. Vermeer went beyond his contemporaries' understanding of light and found new techniques for dealing with it. There is a parallel in this to the struggle of Paul Cézanne, two centuries later, to go beyond the naturalism of the Impressionists. Cézanne looked beneath the appearance of nature to its internal structure. So Vermeer carried the superb realism of Dutch art to a more sublime level by reconciling the various artistic conflicts that limited his contemporaries.

These conflicts involved the problems of dealing with color and perspective, light and dark. For example, aerial perspective, often used by landscapists to indicate depth, required dimming the brilliance of colors until the background was almost monochromatic. Again, in many 17th Century paintings a battle was waged between light and dark: shadows were overemphasized to make the light areas seem lighter. This approach was used by Rembrandt, who often gave strength to his bright centers by plunging the surroundings into darkness.

The wonder of Vermeer is that he succeeded in resolving all these conflicts while remaining within the context of the art of his day. He learned to achieve depth without sacrificing the brightness of his colors. He indicated space with incredibly fine modulations of color, which starts out dark but clear in the farthest corners and becomes gradually brighter and more intense in the light areas until it captures the brilliance of daylight itself. Vermeer often accentuated this light-drenched effect with dazzling little dabs of paint, or *pointillés*, that seem from a distance actually to be made of light.

Vermeer shaded a blue area not by painting brown over blue as most of his contemporaries did, but by using another tone of blue, and then another—each minutely different. These tones accounted for the subtle differences in the color of every surface—differences that depend on its texture, shape and distance from the nearest window or reflection.

The shadows themselves are always variations of color—never black or just brown. Vermeer knew that all shadows have colors, just as he understood that white light is never really white. In an exhaustive study of Vermeer's technique, Swillens studied the white or whitish walls painted by Vermeer, first carefully screening them from their surroundings. He found that although apparently white, each nuance of wall texture, each subtle change of light intensity and tone had been rendered by almost innumerable variations of color—all the colors, in fact, that do exist in the color white.

The sureness of hand and eye required to achieve these effects are almost beyond comprehension. There is still some question as to Vermeer's exact technique. Many modern observers feel he may have used some lens device such as a primitive camera that not only showed perspective clearly but also subtly fused the colors of the scene before him in much the same way that the colors on his canvases are blended.

But whether he used an optical aid or not, it is clear that Vermeer saw more in light and color than did his contemporaries, and that he had an unmatched ability to record with a brush what he saw. In his painting Vermeer was infinitely painstaking, spending months on every picture. As Swillens discovered in his analysis of the paintings, Vermeer's canvases are filled with delicate technical nuances such as "a direction of the brush's stroke, a light groove of the brush hair, an indefinable difference in shade and color, a small surface nearly polished smooth. . . . This layer of paint, sometimes raised to the very minimum, often not wider than a thin silk thread, has its lighted and shadowed side and gives the whole surface . . . an impression of gossamer light."

In achieving this marvelous alchemy, Vermeer resolved another contrast in his century's art. He combined the meticulous rendering of detail of a Gerard Dou with the genius of a Frans Hals for catching the spirit of an instant; though his paintings are the product of endless patience and application, they seem to capture the fleeting essence of light. It has been said that Vermeer conquered reality as a bird conquers gravity. With apparent effortlessness he snatched an instant of reality and lifted it out of a static realism to preserve it in a dynamic world of space, light and color.

Virtuoso of Light

Using many of the same themes—and even many of the same props—as other painters of his day, Vermeer constructed works of art so completely different from theirs, so uniquely his, as to be without parallel either in the 17th Century or in all the years that have flowed away since then. And not the least remarkable thing about his paintings is that, far from being merely charming or exuding an antique air, they go on living, as though each were a split second of eternity.

Unlike other genre painters, Vermeer had no real story to tell, no moral to teach. Nor does he seem to have been particularly imaginative. He had a single goal and he was single-minded about it—finding beauty in the normal, the particular, even the banal. With lenslike precision, he transferred to his canvases the world of the sun-filled room. For Vermeer, light was nature's paintbrush: it not only described the shape of all things but it also bestowed upon them their colors. He approached it reverently. Painting with the motion of neither his arm nor his hand but with the precise movement of his fingers, he blended his pigments so evenly that they have the intensity of colors seen in the ground glass of a camera, and he applied them in layers so thin that they lay like enamel on his canvas. Through the use of techniques like these, he managed, as in the glowing painting opposite, to convey the deep feeling of serenity that is the mark of his work.

Adorning herself with pearls, a girl turns toward a mirror as the light pouring in through the window envelops and transforms her. Within this apparently casual moment of coquetry Vermeer has concealed a deeper connotation of vanity—*vanitas* —the emptiness and brevity of the world of temporal things.

Young Lady Adorning Herself with a Pearl Necklace

128

Pieter de Hoogh: *An Interior, with a Woman Drinking with Two Men, and Maidservant*

From the outset, Vermeer seemed destined to rise above his fellow artists. Even in the early and somewhat self-conscious painting reproduced on the opposite page, in which he has emulated to a large extent the style and anecdotal approach of the popular genre painter Pieter de Hoogh, Vermeer exhibits qualities that De Hoogh could never match. Here, for example, is the light that would become for Vermeer an all-absorbing passion. Streaming in through the casement, it glides across the men and one woman, lingering on sleeves and lace, and making of the simple objects on the table a still life of such sparkling freshness that the painting's faults of execution no longer

HERZOG ULRICH MUSEUM, BRUNSWICK

Couple with a Wine Glass

seem to matter. De Hoogh, one of whose drinking scenes is shown opposite, concerns himself with light, too, but his primary interest is in constructing a viable space in which to set his figures—actors about to put on a little play. De Hoogh seems completely at ease as storyteller, Vermeer not at all. Vermeer unfolds his story of a girl being courted with an almost awkward earnestness. And then, almost as if to compensate for the unnaturalness he feels in staging such a scene, he turns to the things that attract him most —the window, the white jug, the reflected light in the glass, the glint on the brass studs in a Spanish chair—and there, quite clearly, he leaves his heart.

131

Maidservant Pouring Milk

What is so compelling about Vermeer's light? It is, after all, ordinary daylight. But as the art critic Sir Kenneth Clark has pointed out, few artists have bothered to render ordinary daylight in their works, possibly because its tones are cool rather than warm. And even fewer have been the painters like Vermeer who, in Clark's words, based their color harmonies "on the blue, grey, white and pale yellow of a window facing north."

Vermeer's light—as the painting above makes radiantly clear—diffuses itself evenly through space, and, as it does so, it creates its own unerring record, revealing the texture of cloth, bread and wicker, and even picking out nailholes in the whitewashed wall. It obviates the necessity of outline as it flows around objects and gives shape to them. The girl above is defined by light; she stands, as it were, in a nimbus of light. Her blue cuffs and the pleats of her apron fairly scintillate, her white headdress and white collar glow, and in the shadowed folds of her clothing nestle deeper tones of the same cool colors that lend the painting its overall look of subdued richness.

Maidservant Pouring Milk, detail

The Music Lesson

Yet another striking quality of Vermeer's paintings is the perfect order that reigns in them. In the scene above, everything is in its place, and so skillfully have furniture and props been arranged that the room looks much bigger than it is. Utilizing to the fullest this talent for seeing surface pattern and depth at the same time, Vermeer has produced in works like this a total harmony.

This unwavering order and perspective have both intrigued and challenged art historians. The Dutch writer P.T.A. Swillens, for example, analyzing Vermeer's paintings, found it possible to deduce from the sizes of floor tiles the actual measurements of the rooms. Using this information, Swillens plotted the dimensions of the indoor scenes, and he discovered that instead of using several

The Geographer

rooms for his paintings, Vermeer may have worked in only two—the ones shown here. These he made seem infinitely varied with lighting effects, rearranged furniture and props and through the use of curtains and drapes.

Such analysis of Vermeer's work has afforded fascinating insights into his methods of composition, but it has also raised some curious questions. One is how Vermeer, after the faltering beginnings of *The Procuress (page 65)*, could achieve mastery of perspective so soon afterward. Another, even more intriguing, is why the all-important viewing point—that is, the point from which Vermeer observed the scene before him—should so often correspond not to the eye level of a seated or standing man, but, as both of these paintings clearly show, to the level of a window sill.

135

Officer and Laughing C

THE METROPOLITAN MUSEUM OF ART, NEW YORK, BEQUEST OF COLLIS P. HUNTINGTON, 1925

Lady with a Lute

As long ago as 1891, when eyes had not yet grown accustomed to the camera's way of seeing things, Joseph Pennell, an American etcher, lithographer and a friend of Whistler, was struck by the "photographic perspective" of Vermeer's *Officer and Laughing Girl (opposite)*. What had caught his eye was the disproportionate size of the man in relation to the girl. This is the kind of distortion imposed by a camera on objects closest to its lens, and it occurs in many of Vermeer's other works, such as *Lady with a Lute (above)*. Scholars, taking note of it in the 19th Century, often criticized the artist for his failure to reconcile the sizes of figures within a scene and thereby convincingly reduce three-dimensional nature to a two-dimensional image.

Writing about the artist's photographic perspective in the British *Journal of the Camera Club*, Pennell suggested that Vermeer must have employed some sort of mechanical device to help him paint the *Officer and Laughing Girl*. Since then, a growing number of critics have become convinced that Vermeer did in fact utilize a mechanical aid in making at least some of his paintings—a device known as the viewing camera, or camera obscura. This in no way diminishes his integrity—or his art. The camera obscura, a sort of magic lantern in reverse, was a marvel to all those who saw it demonstrated: it caught an image of the real world, through an aperture or a lens, and projected it in a darkened chamber, as a photographic camera today projects an image onto film. Its fascination for an artist like Vermeer in the 17th Century, the age of observation, is self-evident: here was an unimpeachable eye, one that mirrored reality without any of the obfuscations, emotional or otherwise, which becloud human vision. Moreover, it offered a shortcut to perspective. The three-dimensional world could be reduced instantaneously to two dimensions on the camera's screen and could be traced or copied without recourse to the complicated mathematical calculations which artists once employed to work out perspective.

137

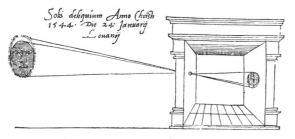

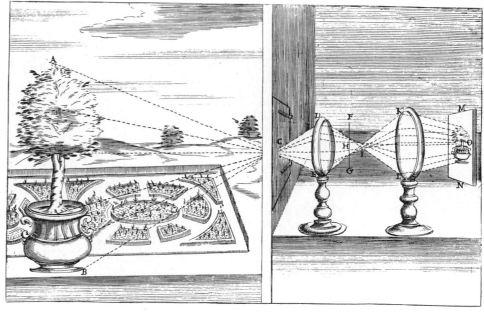

A 1642 diagram of the use of lenses in a camera obscura

Wh   hat sort of camera obscura could Vermeer have used? There were two kinds available to him—the chamber type, consisting of an unlit room with a tiny hole or aperture in one wall through which reflected sunlight could pass, and the portable type, called the *cubiculum*, or little cubicle. The chamber camera obscura had been known even to the ancients, and in the 16th Century a Dutch physician and mathematician had shown, in the illustration at top left, how it could be utilized to observe a solar eclipse without injury to the eye (the viewer stood with his back to the sun and watched the eclipse on the opposite wall). It is entirely possible that Vermeer, in painting the *View of Delft (page 54-55)*, converted the second story of the house in which he worked into a camera obscura—perhaps simply by closing the shutters. He may even have outfitted the necessary aperture with lenses which, as the engraving at center above illustrates,

At its most basic, the camera obscura consists of a darkened room, with a small opening. Reflected images of objects outside enter this hole and are projected on the opposite wall. The image is seen there both upside down and reversed.

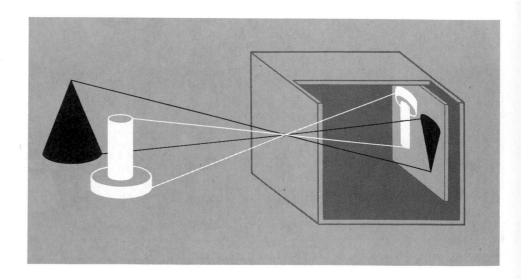

138

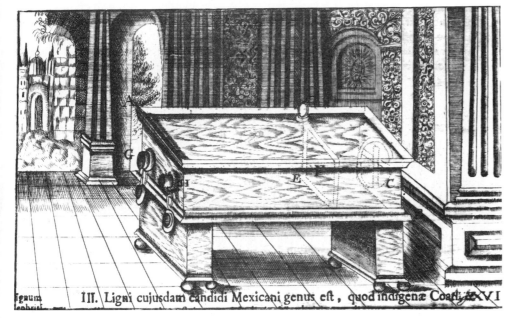

III. Ligni cujusdam candidi Mexicani genus est, quod indigenæ Coatl &XVI

An early portable camera obscura with two lenses

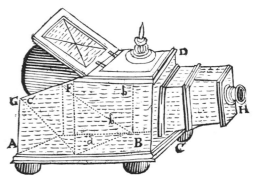

Box-type camera obscura

would have righted what would have been an upside-down image.

While the chamber camera obscura was restricted to outdoor views —and of a single scene at that—the portable type, an innovation of the 17th Century, could be moved about and used both indoors and out. In one of its early forms it resembled a table *(above)* and had two openings —one to look through and the other to let the light in. A subsequent model *(far right)* had an adjustable lens and a slanted metal mirror that projected the image onto a translucent screen. The image could be focused on the screen by moving the lens forward and back slightly. Vermeer may have employed a model like this for some of his indoor scenes. Interestingly, if such a device had been placed on a period table, the height of its lens would have corresponded to the height of the window sills in Vermeer's home—the level of the viewing point in many of his paintings.

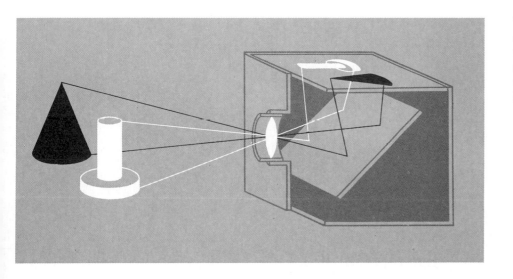

The portable camera obscura, or viewing camera, utilizes a lens to focus and right the image, which is reflected from a slanted mirror to a translucent screen on top of the box. Although righted, the image is still reversed.

View of Delft (detail at left)

One aspect of Vermeer's work that has helped to convince scholars that he did indeed use the camera obscura is his almost uncanny treatment of the play of light on textured surfaces. In the *View of Delft* and in the painting of the girl in a cone-shaped hat he has literally made light sparkle. And upon close examination, the sparkling areas in each can be seen to consist of little dots of flattened paint called *pointillés,* which resemble nothing so much as the fuzzy, overlapping sequins of light that appear in an out-of-focus photograph and are referred to as discs of confusion by photographers. But if they are indeed these, how was it possible for Vermeer to have observed them in nature, since they represent a phenomenon normally not visible to the naked eye? One way he could have seen them is with the camera obscura, in the imperfect image cast by its primitive lenses. If this is so, it is a mark of Vermeer's genius that he could take these dancing points of light and turn them into *pointillés* which set his canvases to shimmering as though sunbeams had been trapped there.

Young Girl with a Flute

The hypothesis that Vermeer used the camera obscura was recently put to the test by Professor Charles Seymour of the Department of Art History at Yale. He drew parallels between Vermeer's painting and photography, by demonstrating, for example, how many of the artist's effects could be reproduced with a camera *(below, left)*. In addition, Seymour took a 19th Century viewing camera obscura (no earlier model was available) and set it up about two-and-a-half feet away from a few carefully chosen props—a chair with lion's head finials, a piece of draped velvet and a tapestry backdrop. When these were viewed on the screen of the camera obscura, they exhibited qualities much like those displayed by similar materials in Vermeer's *Girl with a Red Hat (opposite)*. The lion's head glimmered with discs of confusion, and the fuzzy texture of the velvet was rendered even fuzzier by the soft focus of uncorrected lenses. Even the quality of light and the color tones mirrored Vermeer's own. But it was evident, when a photograph was made duplicating these effects in a polished metal mirror *(below)*, that an all-important ingredient was missing—the artist's selective eye. The secret of Vermeer's art is not that he used the camera obscura but that he used it so well—as a point of departure for art, never as an end in itself.

In sharp focus, the carvings on a picture frame show clearly *(top)*; through an unfocused lens, however, they shimmer in discs of confusion. In the soft-focus photograph at right, a lion's head finial displays qualities of light similar to the finial in the painting opposite.

Girl with a Red Hat

143

144

VII

A Quiet, Compelling Art

A portent of greatness, this early
work by Vermeer contains a
motif he would return to in
several masterpieces, the solitary
act of reading a letter. For the first
time he used what was to become
a favorite device for conveying
depth—a curtain hanging
deceptively parallel to the picture
plane.

*Lady Reading a Letter
at an Open Window*

The study of Vermeer's life yields a few facts, and a scrutiny of his technique is fascinating, but the best way to learn about Vermeer is to examine his paintings. The finest of them, painted during the 10 or 12 years that constituted his major creative period, number not more than 25. Even these, like the artist himself, have an enigmatic reserve that is never completely penetrated. But as one studies them, certain facets of the man and his work are revealed: the subtle development of his art toward simplicity and maturity; his growing preoccupation with the women of his household; proof of his love for the city of Delft; and, perhaps, certain evidence of a lessening of his inspiration. More to the point, one learns to look for the luminous color, the uncanny mastery of light, the unerring balance of design and the strangely arresting stillness that pervade his finest work. In front of Vermeer's pictures, in short, one learns what is important about Vermeer.

One of the most striking things about the small treasure of art Vermeer created during his best years is how little evidence there is in it of the passage of time. Few painters have appeared, after so brief a trial period, with such full-grown mastery of their art. Like his paintings, his genius seems just to be there, without revealing how it developed.

Yet a close examination discloses certain signposts that indicate the maturing of the man and the painter. Consider, for instance, two paintings dealing with the same subject: *Lady Reading a Letter at an Open Window (page 144)* and *Woman in Blue Reading a Letter (page 160)*. The first one is assumed to be an early work, done around 1658; the latter is usually dated six years later. One basis for this chronology is a comparison of the coloring: the earlier picture has warm colors such as browns and red with its complementary green (in the 18th Century, the Dresden Museum, where it still hangs, labeled it a Rembrandt), while the later one shows the dominance of silvery blue and cool yellow, which is particularly characteristic of Vermeer's prime period, the 1660s.

More convincing evidence of the time gap between the two pictures is the classic simplicity of the *Woman in Blue* as compared with the earlier picture. In the *Lady,* Vermeer has used a roomful of artifacts to create his setting: a green-bronze-colored curtain on the right is pulled aside to reveal the scene; on the left a red curtain is draped across an open casement window. In the foreground a Turkish rug and a fruit bowl define depth and space. Within this framework are many color contrasts—the woman's dark dress is set off by bright gold sleeves; the brilliance of the bronze curtain balances the dark window frame.

By comparison, the *Woman in Blue* is a creation of brilliant spareness. Space seems cut off arbitrarily; besides the woman there is nothing in the scene except two chairs, the end of a table with some cloths piled on it and part of a map hanging behind her. The coloring is cool, the only area of brilliance being the warm daylight reflected off the wall. And yet, with this spare furnishing and subdued tonality Vermeer has created a painting that in its introspection and tenderness is stronger and more satisfying than the more complex *Lady.* In this subtle development one clearly senses the maturing of the artist.

Except for two paintings, *The Procuress* and *The Astronomer,* that have dates on them, such internal evidence is all that art historians have to go on in working out a chronology for Vermeer's paintings. In doing this they must to a great extent ignore the possible effects of the chance occurrences of daily life on his work. It is possible, for example, that the heavier coloring of the *Lady* was just an experiment; maybe Vermeer framed her with curtains because he had just bought the green-bronze material and was taken with it; perhaps someone ordered the painting that way and then refused it. Whether likely or unlikely, such mundane influences might have affected Vermeer, and the possibility can only add to scholars' difficulty in determining when he painted what.

It is a mark of the universality of Vermeer's paintings that they can mean all things to all men; thus they pose as many problems of interpretation as of chronology. An intriguing example of this is *The Music Lesson (page 134),* which is tentatively dated about 1662.

Traditionally, critics have agreed that the title of the painting sums up its subject well enough. The two human figures represent student and teacher. They have been relegated to the farthest plane of the picture, where they strike a bold note of dark blue (Vermeer never used unmodulated black) in the softly lit room with its many pastels: blue of the chair, beige of the wall, yellow of the spinet. On the inside of the instrument's cover are the words (with some letters obscured) "Musica Letitiae Co(me)s Medicina Dolor(is)," or "Music is a companion to joy and a cure of sorrow." It is a gentle painting, as private as chamber music, and it portrays a quiet, familiar genre scene.

Perhaps. Some authorities have felt different tensions and seen different meanings in the painting. Lawrence Gowing, a curator at London's Tate Gallery and the author of a standard work on Vermeer, suggests that the gentleman in the painting is not even listening, let alone giving a music lesson. He is, instead, paying court to the young lady. He has just come in from the street, Gowing writes, citing as one proof the fact that the man is still holding his stick. (One could, of course, argue that the stick is a baton used to mark tempo in a music lesson.)

In Gowing's view, the man is awaiting a reply from the lady—and it is one of Vermeer's subtleties not to show her face and therefore not to reveal her reaction. The reflection in the mirror over the spinet shows that she has turned her face slightly toward her caller, but her expression is too undefined to disclose what her answer is; it is only a pattern of light and shadow. The mirror thus becomes, in Gowing's words, "the private heart of the picture," and the issue is "held in perpetual suspense." (Vermeer also used the gossamer reflection of a woman's face with telling effect in the *Lady Reading a Letter at an Open Window.*)

Once one has read this interpretation, it is hard to shake it off. It is clear that Vermeer was fascinated by the mysteries of love and desire. Perhaps part of the magic of this haunting picture lies in a feeling that the woman is about to decide the fate of her pale, motionless suitor.

Various interpretations have also been advanced for the *Girl Asleep (page 8).* Its present title suggests a simple genre scene of an idle servant girl. But in the 1696 Amsterdam auction catalogue, the picture was described as showing "a drunken, sleeping girl at a table." The theme was a familiar one at the time, and the presence of a wineglass and what appears to be an overturned carafe undoubtedly led to the interpretation of drunkenness.

But still another meaning has been read into the work. Faintly visible in the obscure background of the painting is a picture of Cupid (only the left leg shows), with a mask lying on the ground. Vermeer sometimes played allegorical games with his viewers, in the fashion of the day, and to the audience of the time Cupid often symbolized disappointed love. So perhaps the girl is neither drunk nor sleeping, but lost in sad reverie.

There is no final answer to these conjectures. Other genre artists of the day explained in their paintings what was happening and what was about to happen. None of them left so many ambiguities and tantalizing questions as Vermeer. He tells nothing because he was painting not to amuse an audience but to express himself in terms of color, shape and mood. Very probably, Vermeer, if he could be questioned about it, would say that his paintings mean whatever one wants them to mean.

There are some Vermeer paintings in which the problem of interpretation does not really exist, because they are so simple, so private, that one is not even tempted to search for a story. These are his paintings showing a single figure, a woman, engaged in some domestic activity. Most were probably painted when the artist was in his early thirties, and, while all generalizations about Vermeer are subject to exceptions, it seems fair to say that these paintings are the most admired part of his work.

One of the first of these, done about 1663, is the *Young Woman with a Water Jug (pages 17, 27).* In this painting Vermeer worked with the cool simplicity of form and color that is evident in the *Woman in Blue Reading a Letter,* painted about a year later. Blue is the dominant tone; it is the color of the woman's dress and the material on the chair, and it is delicately worked into the shaded side of her headdress, into the wall behind her, even into the light that comes through the window. (One authority has noted that probably no glass in Vermeer's time was completely colorless.) The shadows under the window sill are subtly graduated, the folds in the woman's headdress are exquisitely delineated, the reflection of

During his 40-year study of Vermeer, historian P.T.A. Swillens examined every document relating to the artist's life and, as part of an extensive survey of Vermeer's techniques, he drew the room reconstructions below of *The Geographer (above)*, and other interiors. From his diagrams, Swillens calculated Vermeer's eye level *(line O-H)* and concluded, among other things, that the artist painted while seated, and that he was about five feet seven inches tall. Other scholars *(pages 134-135)* have used the same evidence to deduce that Vermeer may have employed a mechanical aid.

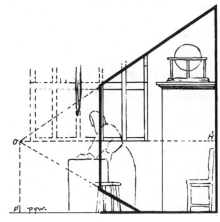

Hypothetical side view

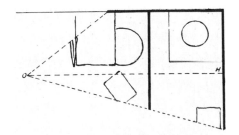

Hypothetical top view

the Turkish rug in the silver bowl is superb. The woman's pose is a simple one, but Vermeer has invested it with dignity and charm.

About 1665 Vermeer painted the *Lady Weighing Gold (page 153)*. The pregnant woman is perhaps, once again, Catharina Vermeer. She wears a deep-blue jacket bordered with ermine, as was fashionable for ladies of that time. (This jacket reappears in other paintings in yellow; the woman's headcloth is almost exactly the same as that worn by the woman with the water jug.) She is testing her scales; before her on the table are various articles that would be found in a goldsmith's shop.

On the wall behind the woman hangs a painting of the Last Judgment, and Vermeer surely did not choose that picture by chance. Here again, as in the *Girl Asleep,* is a subtle allegorical note that adds an extra ingredient to the work, without in the slightest way disturbing its purity. The Last Judgment quietly suggests there is more in the act of the girl than merely the adjusting of scales. It lends a mystical gleam to her weighing, to her holding a balance, leading to thoughts of the balance in which men's souls are held. It has also been pointed out that the picture contains some *vanitas* elements: the gold and pearls, the mirror and the scales.

Even without such incidental elements it is clear that this is not just a picture of a tradeswoman preparing for business. The dreamy gentleness in her face and lowered eyes, the delicacy of her fine hands express a much fuller meaning of beauty and tenderness. And even this interpretation is unnecessary in the inexhaustible world of Vermeer—it is possible simply to enjoy the exquisite play of colors as one would delight in the sight of a field of flowers.

A painting strongly reminiscent of the *Lady Weighing Gold* is the *Young Lady Adorning Herself with a Pearl Necklace (page 129).* This work changed hands in Amsterdam in 1811 for the equivalent of about $15 and later was the prize of Thoré-Bürger's collection. Vermeer shows us the same room as in the *Lady Weighing Gold,* but now it is luminous with daylight; yellow rather than blue is the dominant hue, and the wall is almost white. This girl is lost in contemplation, too, but she is simply and happily contemplating herself as she puts on a necklace before the mirror.

In the *Maidservant Pouring Milk (pages 132-133),* there is little contemplation, but great stillness. This intense work also portrays a single female figure, but it was probably painted several years before the three works just discussed, and contains no trace of allusion. It shows only a maid pouring milk into a pot: a physical presence recorded by the artist, a capturing of reality that even includes a nail hole in the wall.

But as Vermeer watched the colors of the scene come to life in the light from the window, he must have undergone a sudden, overwhelming intensification of feeling. For here, in this modest room, he has brought time to a halt. It is not just any moment, but one chosen, unforgettable moment. Life offers such moments, too; everyone carries in his mind a few etched-in images—of a sunny morning walk on a beach, perhaps, and a confrontation with little birds strutting in the sand; or of an afternoon in childhood, coming out of school at dusk. No one can say why this moment and not another is so memorable. But it was Vermeer's genius to create a number of these moments, and to preserve them.

The simplest of this series of single figures is the charming *Girl in a Turban (page 161),* showing only the head and one shoulder of a young girl. She wears a blue and yellow headdress and a yellow-green jacket, or cape. This was unusual dress for the time, and Vermeer may have deliberately bedecked his model in old-fashioned clothes; or the costume may have been playfully improvised. The girl, who is very young, might even have been one of his daughters. Her eyes, her slightly open mouth, her soft lips all combine to make a portrait of superlative quality.

The girl's pearl eardrop, besides emphasizing Vermeer's love of that substance, exemplifies his genius for using the play of light to define matter. If the canvas is examined at close range, the eardrop appears to have no outline, no shape of pearl; it is just a few dabs of paint. Yet so cunningly are they applied that when seen from a distance they fuse into an image with a texture and luminosity that describe the pearl precisely.

Girl in a Turban hangs in the Mauritshuis in The Hague, having been presented by a collector who bought it in 1882 for less than the cost of a reproduction of it today. (The price was low even for that time, because of the very bad condition of the painting. It has been restored, which involved repairing a hole under the girl's left eye and one on her left cheekbone.) The Mauritshuis is an old and quiet little museum, and provides a perfect setting for *Girl in a Turban.* On a winter day, there may be no one in the room where it hangs. The streets outside lie silent; the light from the low Dutch sky is as Vermeer knew it. And, amid all the elaborate 17th Century pieces around her—landscapes, interiors, large linens—this girl stands out clearly and dominates the room.

The 1696 auction catalogue listed three townscapes by Vermeer, and two of these have survived: *View of Delft (pages 54-55)* and *Street in Delft (page 56).* They have been known as Vermeers as far back as they can be traced. The *View* has been called by some observers the most beautiful town scene ever painted.

The place from which *View of Delft* was painted can be fairly closely determined: at a window on the second floor of a building that stood across the River Schie from the port of Delft. The view from there today is cluttered with new buildings and a large natural-gas reservoir, but the structure of the old town is still there, and so is the water; the boats seem not to have changed their shapes at all. For esthetic effect Vermeer altered the view by moving some buildings around, but that in no way diminished the intrinsic realism of the work. Indeed, standing there today under a sky swept with clouds, one undergoes an overwhelming sense of continuity with the past of 300 years ago.

In Vermeer's *View* there is a touch of the Middle Ages; and there is much in it of Delft—and its light—as it still is today. Each detail stands out with extraordinary brightness; the elusive, bright light that comes just before a storm has been perfectly captured. But, above all, it expresses the essence of Vermeer's Delft; it is the document of a great artist's love for his birthplace.

How different from the powerful simplicity of the *View of Delft* are some of the paintings generally thought to have been the works of Vermeer's later years! All Dutch painting was suffering from a loss of inspiration as the Golden Age came to a close, and it is possible that even the genius of Vermeer was affected. Whether that was the case or whether Vermeer was merely experimenting, these later works are in a different mood. They are of rather elaborate structure, and sometimes show sharper color contrasts than in the earlier works.

One such picture, usually dated about 1670, is *The Love Letter (page 158)*, showing a lady accepting a letter from her maid—a familiar subject for Vermeer. There are other Vermeerian touches, too: the blue and yellow harmony of colors, the brass-knobbed chair, the music, the curtain, the tiles. But there are uncharacteristic notes, as well. First, one has a strong temptation to make a typical genre interpretation of the situation: the maid seems to be looking down with a knowing smile, the lady looking up at her warningly (perhaps even worriedly), as if defying the maid to show that she knows it is a love letter she has just handed her mistress. This is more of a story than Vermeer usually tells.

Furthermore, the structure of the painting—with the small room in the foreground opening into a bigger room—is much more complex than in most Vermeer works. There is a staginess, an over-rich quality about the painting that contradicts the simple genius of earlier works.

Vermeer's last work is usually considered to be the *Allegory of the New Testament (pages 162-163)*, painted perhaps in 1672, at just about the time he moved from his house, Mechelen. The work has also been called an "Allegory of the Catholic Faith," for it is a more or less free interpretation of a symbolic description of that faith as given in a contemporary book of "Iconology . . . Virtues, Vices, Human Passions, Arts, Doctrines." This work, popular with scholars in those days, explained in great detail the traditional religious symbolism of different objects and artifacts. Many of these appear in Vermeer's painting. But, aside from telling its allegory about the triumph of the faith and of good over evil, the work has little to say, at least for a Vermeer. The figure of Faith, her right foot propped on a globe, has been portrayed with the most impersonal face Vermeer ever did. The construction is stiff, the scene cluttered and, except for such touches as the curtain and hanging glass ball, there is little of Vermeer's customary luminous color harmony. Perhaps the painting was done on commission or for a civic occasion; in any case, it was not a picture born in his private, secret world—which is precisely why it has very few admirers now.

The other allegory painted by Vermeer, however, is one of his finest works. It is *An Artist in His Studio (pages 164-167)*, which is usually dated about 1670, though some experts put it earlier. This is the painting that Catharina Vermeer transferred to her mother in partial settlement of a debt in 1675 and which was later threatened by bankruptcy sale.

The work has had an even more adventurous recent past. It was sold as a De Hoogh in 1813 to a Viennese aristocrat, Count Czernin, by a saddler for the equivalent of about $10. In the 1860s Thoré-Bürger authenticated it as a Vermeer. For more than a century the Czernin family kept the painting (it had been on loan for some years to the Kunsthis-

One of the many irksome problems facing Vermeer scholars is the fact that the artist rarely signed his paintings the same way twice; the seven signatures shown here are but a few of many believed to be genuine. All attempts to date his works by his signature have failed.

torisches Museum in Vienna), refusing other art collectors' offers that are said to have gone as high as two million dollars.

But finally a collector with more persuasive methods broke the family's resolve. Adolf Hitler, after applying pressure and perhaps even threats of force, acquired the painting in 1940 at a price of several hundred thousand dollars. He bought it for a museum which he dreamed of establishing, after victory, in his mother's honor in the Austrian town of Linz. Labeled simply "A. H., Linz," the painting was hidden away with 6,750 other works of art in a salt mine in the mountains near Salzburg when the Allies found it in 1945. It is now back in the Vienna Museum.

For Vermeer lovers, *An Artist in His Studio* alone makes a trip to Vienna worthwhile. It is a large canvas—about 52 by 43 inches—showing a painter at his easel just beginning to fill in the color of a laurel wreath worn by his model. She also wears a stiff silk drapery, and holds a trumpet and a golden book. There is a mask on the table and a map of the Netherlands behind her.

The model represents either Fame or Clio, the muse of history, and she tells of the glory of both the Netherlands and of Dutch art. But this vague symbolism loses its importance in the face of the inspired artistry of the painting itself. Every detail, every touch of paint contributes to its impact, from the knobs on the chair in the foreground to the highlights on the bronze chandelier; from the painstaking reproduction of the detailed little panoramas around the wall map to the demure expression of the girl who is posing.

This painting, unlike the *Allegory of the New Testament,* shows all the elements of color, structure and content working together. It is not a simple picture; it is quite busy. And it has an odd aspect, with the painter, in his bizarre jacket and drooping leggings, planted firmly on his stool, back to the viewer. But in studying the picture, one sees that the complexity is natural and unmannered, and that the dynamic pose of the artist is precisely what makes the painting come alive.

In mood, it is far from the simplicity of Vermeer's exquisite portrayals of single female figures. But in its own compelling way it sums up the genius of Vermeer. In showing a painter at work—it may or may not be Vermeer himself—it reproduces the world that Vermeer understood best, the world of the studio. The scene is full of familiar elements: the blue and yellow color harmony; the delicate nuances of color in the shadows; the absolutely convincing way the figures and objects occupy their places in the whole; the clear light flooding in from the left finely modeling every object and surface.

The familiar ambiguity is also present: is it a half-humorous self-portrait? Is this Vermeer's own studio? What is the full meaning of the allegory? Finally, there is the stillness that is Vermeer's special hallmark; the magical hesitation of time that isolates the scene in a light-filled moment of calm.

Of this work, one critic has remarked that "if it is not his supreme masterpiece, it is his most complex and famous work." Another, more significantly, wrote that only when he stood in front of *An Artist in His Studio* were his eyes fully opened to the meaning of Vermeer.

The Poet of Domesticity

Although Vermeer may have had no real anecdotes to relate, no moral messages to deliver in his works, he never failed to fill his paintings with poetic meanings. At first glance, this masterpiece may seem to represent little more than a woman weighing pearls and gold—and indeed it can be appreciated on that level alone. But a deeper probing of the painting, with an awareness of the importance attached to symbolism in Vermeer's time, reveals that it is an allegory of the subtlest sort. Here, as in almost all else that he did, Vermeer has painted nothing simply by chance. Pearls, gold, scales, the picture on the wall, the woman herself—all relate to one another and all are part of the idea he wished to express.

The key that unlocks the allegory is the scene of the Last Judgment in the background. Immediately an analogy becomes apparent between God judging the just and the unjust and the woman weighing gold. The gold and the pearls spilling from the strongbox now acquire another meaning: they represent everything that mortal man values and tries vainly, in the face of his mortality, to hold on to. And yet despite these allusions to death, the painting is not depressing. On the contrary, it is filled with hope, for the woman is pregnant. Standing there with scale in hand, a focus of calm in a twilight glow, she makes clear Vermeer's intention —the celebration of life everlasting.

Dressed according to the fashions of the 1660s in a fur-trimmed jacket as protection against the damp cold, Vermeer's model nevertheless has the otherworldly look of a religious subject. The man who auctioned this picture after Vermeer's death described it, accurately, as "extraordinarily clever and powerfully painted."

A Lady Weighing Gold (Pearls)

153

At the center of Vermeer's world were women, and at the center of their world lay the pearl. The girl writing a letter at right and the girl with the moon-pale face looking so affectingly out of the portrait *(below)* both wear pearl eardrops. So do almost all of Vermeer's other sitters. Within the shimmering circumference of these pendant jewels all Vermeer's light seems concentrated. Who the girls were nobody will ever know. Perhaps they were his daughters. As with the other women he painted, he has not allowed his brush to lie—neither girl is pretty. Yet in his appreciation of them, whoever they may have been, he has given them something of the milky sheen, the luster of the pearls they so proudly possess. And such is the force of his talent that when seen in the overall context of the works of which they are so important a part, they appear beautiful.

Head of a Young Woman

A Lady Writing

The Concert

Three themes run with insistence through Vermeer's work—letter-writing, letter-reading and music-making. He must have been attracted to them for a simple reason: they gave him the chance to paint a conveniently recognizable activity without having to put undue emphasis on the activity and thus subvert the total harmony of effect he was after. It is no accident that the women in the paintings at right are not even shown playing their instruments. And in *The Concert (opposite)*, the man and women have been viewed from such a distance as to suggest that what they are doing is less important than the way they dispose themselves as parts of the composition.

The unobtrusiveness of Vermeer's models is fully in keeping with his purpose: character would have drawn too much attention to itself and motion would have fractured the absolute stillness of the moment. But almost as though he sensed that to pursue this goal to its ultimate conclusion would leave his paintings cold, Vermeer threaded through them yet another theme—love. Most often it is present in only the most oblique fashion. For example, on the wall of the room opposite hangs Baburen's *Procuress (page 67)*. In its venality, it comments wittily on the action that transpires in front of it, hinting that perhaps beneath the quiet exteriors of Vermeer's man and woman there lurk stronger passions.

And so it is with the two paintings at right. In the one at the top, a picture of Cupid holding a letter aloft in the background seems to allude to the true nature of the teacher-pupil relationship. In the other painting the same picture does much the same thing, suggesting that the woman standing at the virginal may be thinking of—or looking at—her lover.

Girl Interrupted at Her Music

Lady Standing at a Virginal

The Love Letter

Vermeer's predilection for the device of the picture within a picture gets one of its fullest expressions in this painting, in which a love-struck woman is about to open a letter brought by a maid. The canvases on the wall—a landscape and a seascape—suggest that the letter writer may be far away, as does the map hanging in the shadows to the left of the door. But fond as Verméer was of such allusions, he seems not to have used any at all in the

Lady Writing a Letter with Her Maid

somewhat later painting above, almost as though he wanted it to be accepted on its own terms only. There is no connection—at least none has yet been made—between the subject of the painting in the background, the finding of Moses, and that of Vermeer's painting, the writing of a letter. Thus the viewer is drawn back to an appreciation of the artist's underlying purpose—posing simply grouped figures and letting light paint the scene.

159

Woman in Blue Reading a Letter

Among the simplest and loveliest of all Vermeer's paintings are the two shown here. To take them apart and analyze them, however, is to be baffled by them. The face of the girl in the turban was built up, as radiographs have revealed, almost from light itself: there are not the faintest traces of lines to be seen anywhere, either below the surface of the painting or on it. And here the luminous yellow and limpid blue of Vermeer conspire for a magical effect.

Much the same blue turns the jacket of the woman above into a living garment. Another Dutch artist, Van Gogh, found himself drawn to this painting at a time when few knew Vermeer. "This strange painter's palette," he said in amazement at the choice of color, "consists of blue, lemon yellow, pearl gray, black and white."

Girl in a Turban

Allegory of the New Testament

After the understated poetry of his masterpieces, the overt symbolism and the flamboyant pose of Virtue in the allegorical painting at left seem to mark a new and strange departure in Vermeer's career. Certainly this has contributed to its being one of the least appreciated of his works, although, as these details show, it contains much that is beautiful and even striking. One reason why it appears so out of character is that Vermeer based it on a literary source, a famous book of symbolism by an Italian knight.

Although called *Allegory of the New Testament*, the painting is actually an allegory of the Catholic faith. Dressed in pure white, with hand clasped over her bosom to indicate where "the true and living Faith rests," Virtue stands with one foot planted triumphantly on a globe symbolizing the earth. In the foreground lie Evil, crushed under a cornerstone, and the apple "whereby sin is caused." But perhaps the most intriguing aspect of the painting is the glimpse it provides of Vermeer's working world—the room, with its curtains partially drawn, reflected dimly in the glass ball. Hidden somewhere in the darkness must be Vermeer himself.

Allegory of the New Testament, detail

Allegory of the New Testament, detail

Allegory of the New Testament, detail

An Artist in His Studio

164

An Artist in His Studio, detail

Symbols are so well married to content and mood in what many consider to be Vermeer's masterpiece that it was long known by the realistic title *An Artist in His Studio*. Modern scholarship, however, has revealed that the picture conceals a meaning of its own, and that is why it is now often called the *Allegory of Fame*. The artist seated at his easel is portraying Fame. The map of Holland, emblazoned with coats of arms *(above)* and replete with the ships that had helped make the country rich and a home of art, suggests that the Lowlands had become the new Parnassus, and that because of the achievements of Dutch artists, Fame, wearing a laurel wreath, has taken up her residence there. But in the end, it is not the allegory that makes the painting unforgettable but the picture's clean, clear light, its beauty of color, and the insouciance of the young girl who serves as the model *(detail, overleaf)*.

165

168

VIII

A Legacy
of Mystery

This early Vermeer seems to
point to a religious phase in the
artist's career. Acting on this
possibility the 20th Century
Dutch forger Han van Meegeren
proceeded to paint a series of
"lost" religious Vermeers, which
fooled many for a time.

*Christ in the House of
Mary and Martha*

So much uncertainty surrounds the history of Vermeer's paintings that
it is tempting to hope that someday a cache of them will be discovered
in some attic or forgotten storeroom. But the hope probably is vain.
Considering how slowly he worked and remembering that he lived in a
houseful of children and ran an art dealership besides, one should perhaps be surprised that he produced as many known works as he did.

The difficulty is, no one really can be sure how many paintings he did
produce. Ever since Thoré-Bürger published his list of more than 70
Vermeers in 1866, art historians, dealers and collectors have argued end-
lessly about the authenticity of some of the paintings attributed to Vermeer. During the recent past, the range has narrowed so that there are
only a few paintings still labeled "Vermeer?" with that tantalizing question mark. Even so, estimates by the most respected authorities as to
the number of undoubted Vermeers vary from 29 to 36.

The problem is a prickly one, because the authorship of a Vermeer
painting is seldom a simple matter to decide. First there is the problem of
signature. Vermeer signed his name or monogram in at least half a dozen
different ways, and time and damage to canvases have made many of the
signatures almost impossible to decipher. Some of the paintings believed to be by Vermeer are simply unsigned. Furthermore, the practice
of some art dealers of selling various artists' works under the names of
other painters to get better prices has cast doubt on many signatures.
Often a cleaning shows that a signature was added long after the original painting was executed.

In assessing the authorship of any painting of the 17th Century, it
is also important to remember that many of them, including Vermeer's,
changed hands during the 18th and 19th Centuries at prices that made
them of less value to their owners than a good suit or a Sunday dress.
It is not in the least surprising that they were treated with little respect
—that backgrounds were sometimes painted over, objects and figures
changed according to the owner's taste and pieces cut off to make them
fit a frame or particular niche. An 18th Century owner of a Vermeer
would not have thought a great deal more about hiring another painter

appeared in art periodicals. It was given routine tests for age and passed them all. Most European experts quickly agreed with Dr. Bredius, and the few dissenting voices—such as that of Professor Johan Huizinga of Leiden University, who said the work was "lacking in soul and only playing with colors"—were ignored. The painting was acquired by a museum in Rotterdam for $286,000. Critics raved. One noted that it showed evidence of Vermeer's "favorite balance of pale blues and yellows," and added that the face of Christ was "infinitely pathetic and benign." A Dutch museum director wrote that the serving maid in *Emmaus* had the most beautiful face ever painted by Vermeer.

A dramatic turn of fate brought Van Meegeren's deception to light. He had followed *Emmaus* with five other forged Vermeers (plus two fake De Hooghs). One of the "Vermeers" was acquired during World War II by Hermann Goering, whose art-collecting zeal surpassed Hitler's; as a result of this transaction Van Meegeren was charged after the war with treasonable collaboration with the enemy for his part in the loss of a Dutch national treasure to the Nazis.

Van Meegeren had intended to take his secret to the grave and reveal the truth only in his will. But now his deception had placed him in serious trouble, and in July 1945, after six weeks of detention, he announced the truth: not only were the Goering picture and *Emmaus* not national treasures, they were not even Vermeers. They were fakes, and he, Han van Meegeren, had painted them.

At first no one believed him. But as a battery of scientific tests was brought to bear on the *Emmaus,* the experts gradually and reluctantly began to credit Van Meegeren's statements. To support his case, the forger had volunteered to paint *another* "Vermeer" under the eyes of the authorities. He actually started on this work, but after two months he learned that the collaboration charge was to be changed to forgery, and he thereupon refused to finish the new counterfeit work.

Van Meegeren was brought to trial on October 29, 1947, after more than two years of preparation. The trial was sensational but brief: it took just one day; he was found guilty and sentenced to a year in jail for deliberate fraud; he died of a heart attack before he started serving the sentence, but his dramatic hoax was not soon forgotten. Art critics and experts, shaken by the affair, still shudder at the name of Van Meegeren.

The aspect of the great forgery that seems most astonishing today is not that *Emmaus* almost managed to pass the scientists' scrutiny, but that art critics of high reputation should have judged it to be a Vermeer—and a great Vermeer at that. Opinion is still divided as to whether *Emmaus* is a good painting or not. Some critics find it handsome, many others think it ugly—"The Emmaus is *dead,*" wrote André Malraux. But almost no one today thinks it looks like a Vermeer. The faces are heavy lidded and hollow cheeked; the rendering of the hands is weak; the folds in the disciples' sleeves are unconvincing.

Undoubtedly a kind of mass hypnosis was at work when the critics of the 1930s were taken in; it should be remembered that many experts were very anxious to find new Vermeers. And unquestionably some of the critics were influenced by the carefully forged signature and by what other critics had to say about the picture. As one observer has put it, they looked with their ears and not their eyes—and this was precisely what Van Meegeren was trying to prove. In a way, it is hard not to feel some sympathy for his act.

Today's viewers of the *Emmaus* have difficulty understanding how it ever passed as a Vermeer in the 1930s—and this emphasizes one of the chief differences between great art and indifferent art. A good painting continues to have meaning through all time. Different generations find different values in it, but its worth is timeless. A bad painting loses its impact quickly as tastes change. A forgery the public of the 1930s thought looked like a Vermeer no longer does now. A forger of Vermeer today would have to try completely different techniques to be successful, because in many subtle ways Vermeer looks different to us today. After 10 or 20 years, today's forgery would, in its turn, be hard to understand— while the art it imitated or resembled would continue to be meaningful.

The reason Vermeer continues to have meaning so long after his own day is that while his work was to a great extent the product of his time, it was not painted *for* his time. Vermeer painted to satisfy himself, and the exquisite artistic taste and style that guided him are not bound to any one era or generation. The essentially uninteresting subject matter of Vermeer's pictures is irrelevant—how he saw his subjects and how he painted are what count.

The clarity and sensitivity of his vision made Vermeer an inspiration to many Impressionist painters, and it was on them, of all modern artists, that he has had the most direct influence. They were deeply impressed by his understanding of light and color. Renoir said that he considered *The Lace Maker (page 120)* one of the best pictures in the world, and he is supposed to have felt a lifelong regret at not ever having gone to Vienna to see Vermeer's *An Artist in His Studio.*

In the past 50 years Vermeer's impact has spread to an increasingly enthusiastic public. Crowds flock to see his pictures, and reproductions are bought in great quantity. A major art event of 1966 was the exhibition of paintings entitled "In the Light of Vermeer" that drew enormous crowds and critical acclaim in The Hague and Paris. The exhibit included 11 Vermeers, the largest number gathered in one place since the Amsterdam auction of 1696.

Art historians are more fascinated than ever by the mystery of Vermeer's life, and experts devote monographs to discussions of his works, to the question of whether he used a camera obscura and to the problem of the attribution of various paintings—debates that may never be fully resolved.

But no amount of historical research or psychological analysis will ever remove the provocative ambiguities that surround him. The air of enigma is an essential quality in his work. There is a reserve that can never be broached. This makes it hard to understand or fully know Vermeer, but it is at the core of his eternal fascination.

If the mystery of Vermeer endures, so does his genius. Serene, luminous, delicately balanced, the poetry of Vermeer's art is impervious to time. Silent, intense in his light-filled studio, the Master of Delft moves us still.

A Forger's Postscript to Vermeer

The pensive figure in the lower right-hand corner of this photograph is Han van Meegeren—the man who presumed himself to be the equal of Vermeer and who is remembered today as one of the most successful art forgers of all time. He is shown here awaiting trial in 1946 and musing over two of his own works, a maudlin canvas of a widow with her brood and a small picture called *The Street Singers*. He had hoped to achieve fame with paintings like these, to which his own name was signed, but the expected praise did not come. Then he saw another way: "Spurred by the disappointment of receiving no acknowledgment from artists and critics . . . I determined to prove my worth as a painter by making a perfect 17th Century canvas." And such was the force of his will and his technical skill that he succeeded in producing not one but six paintings that passed as Vermeers as well as two convincing "De Hooghs."

Van Meegeren's story, for all its fascination, is a sad one. He had mistaken himself for a genius—a Vermeer —when in fact he lacked the inspiration, the authentically personal vision of the artist he sought to emulate. But his unfortunate story has value: in the study and analysis of Van Meegeren's forgeries modern art scholarship took an important step forward. The unprecedented investigation called for the combined skills of the art historian, the esthetician, the chemist and the physicist, it has become a classic example of science serving art.

Master-forger Han van Meegeren stares up at a picture he painted in the 1940s. It bears a strong compositional resemblance to the third of his Vermeer forgeries, the *Last Supper (pages 180-181)*.

174

Woman Drinking, Hals style, 1935-1936

Portrait of a Man, Terborch style, 1935-1936

Interior with Drinkers, De Hoogh style, 1937-1938

Once Van Meegeren had made up his mind to paint a perfect 17th Century canvas, he faced a difficult decision: which master was he to copy? He experimented with a variety of styles, as the paintings shown here indicate. At left is a "De Hoogh," which Van Meegeren actually sold—perhaps with some amusement, since he had once bought a fake De Hoogh himself. The "Terborch" above and the "Hals" next to it he kept, possibly because he did not feel that they would pass the test of a critical eye.

Van Meegeren's warm-up exercise for his effort in Vermeer's style may have been the painting opposite: it is a composite of several works, the model drawn from *Woman in Blue Reading a Letter (page 160).* But as any comparison will quickly show, it is quite a poor imitation. The pearl eardrop lacks the opalescent sheen that Vermeer would have given it, *pointillés* appear in the hair where Vermeer would not have put them, and the jacket, hanging in stiff creases and leaden swags, has none of the softness, the naturalness of the original. In spite of this, Van Meegeren decided to forge Vermeers. To mask his inadequacies, he cleverly chose to concentrate not on Vermeer's domestic style, but on religious subjects known from one early painting.

Woman Reading Music, Vermeer style, 1935-1936

Han van Meegeren: *Christ and the Disciples at Emmaus,* 1936-1937

The painting reproduced above is Van Meegeren's greatest "Vermeer," *Christ and the Disciples at Emmaus.* Whatever one may think of it as a work of art (and many people found it beautiful indeed), it is certainly a technical tour de force. Van Meegeren spent four years working out techniques for making a new painting look old. The biggest problem he faced was getting his oil paint to harden thoroughly—a process that normally takes 50 years. He solved it by mixing his pigments with a synthetic resin instead of oil, and baking the canvas.

Now he was ready to begin. He took an actual 17th Century painting and removed most of the picture with pumice and water, being most careful not to obliterate the network of cracks, which, as will be seen, had an important role to play. But a patch of white paint failed to come off, and Van Meegeren was forced to build his composition around it. Almost all that had been white in the old painting he made white in the new—the

tablecloth. A small area to the left of the water jug he could no nothing with and he painted it over. Years later X-rays *(opposite)* would reveal a ghostlike head in the area above Christ's left hand.

Just how well Van Meegeren succeeded with his deception is shown in a statement by a leading Dutch scholar: "We have here a—I am inclined to say—*the* masterpiece of Johannes Vermeer of Delft." Indeed, no protesting voices were heard until eight years later, in 1945, when Van Meegeren was charged with having collaborated with the Nazis by selling them Dutch art treasures. His incredible confession that he only sold art he painted himself touched off a two-year investigation. During that probing, a complete scientific analysis of the new "Vermeers" was made under the direction of Dr. P. B. Coremans, head of the Central Laboratories of the Belgian Museums, whose team produced the technical evidence shown on this and the following pages.

Caravaggio: *Supper at Emmaus*, 1606

Han van Meegeren: Sketch of *Christ and the Disciples at Emmaus*

Van Meegeren may have used the composition of a Caravaggio *(above)* as the basis for his forgery. This was canny; scholars had always suspected that Vermeer had a connection with Italy and the "lost painting" confirmed this. So convinced were they that they could not believe Van Meegeren's confession that the picture was fake. As proof, he made the sketch at left, showing a head *(circled)* he had been unable to remove from the old canvas. Though a radiograph *(below)* showed the head to be left, not right, of the jug, the sketch made clear that Van Meegeren's story was essentially true—he had indeed painted the "Vermeer."

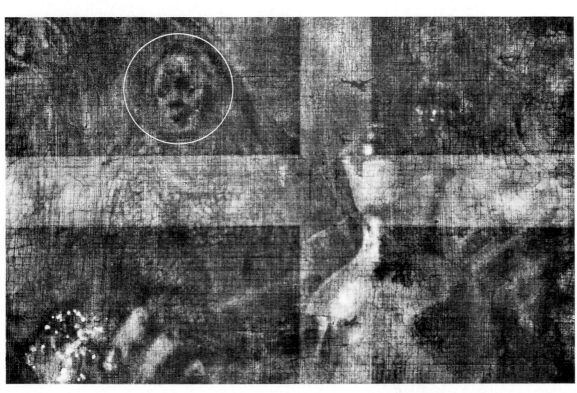

Christ and the Disciples at Emmaus, radiograph of detail

During the investigation, Van Meegeren revealed that having once fooled the art world with *Christ and the Disciples at Emmaus* he was encouraged to try new forgeries. He painted a head of Christ, sold it through an intermediary and then "found" the *Last Supper (below)* for which it was a supposed study. The buyer of the Christ was only too eager to snap up the full-scale painting.

Perhaps the greatest problem that faced Van Meegeren then was the secrecy in which he had to work. He could hire no models, since they might talk. For the painting below he was forced to rely mainly on his imagination,

and it is a wonder that he dared such a complicated composition, involving 13 figures in a variety of poses. At one point he stole directly from Vermeer, using the head in the *Girl in a Turban* for his head of St. John, as the paired photographs at left show. Van Meegeren was even so bold as to draw upon one of his own earlier works for the face of the wraithlike disciple seated between the two standing figures at the left in the painting.

Amazingly, this painting, so obviously inferior to the first "newly discovered Vermeer," was grabbed up as greedily as the other. But with Van Meegeren's success

had come carelessness, perhaps bred of the contempt he felt for "experts" who could be gulled so easily. This time he had not even bothered to remove the 17th Century hunting scene from the canvas on which he had overpainted the *Last Supper*. Inexplicably, the radiographs that would have detected the forgery instantly were not made. Later, during the examination before his trial, a radiograph *(below)* clearly showed the old picture. An interesting sidelight was provided still later, when an art dealer turned up a photograph *(bottom, right)* of the old canvas, which he recalled having sold to Van Meegeren.

Last Supper, detail of radiograph

Han van Meegeren: *Last Supper*, 1940-1941

Abraham Hondius: *Hunting Scene*

The final irony in the strange tale of Van Meegeren is that when at last he was caught, he was charged initially not as a forger, but as a collaborator. What had helped to seal his fate was the sale of his fifth signed "Vermeer" to Field-Marshal Goering by an art dealer. That painting—*Woman Taken in Adultery*—may be seen on the opposite page as it was hung, unframed, during Van Meegeren's trial. One of the poorest of his forgeries, it nevertheless fetched the highest price of any—and part of the arrangement whereby it was sold to Goering involved the return to Holland of some 200 works of Dutch art looted earlier in the War by the Nazis.

In order to clear himself of the charge of collaboration and claim his long-overdue fame, Van Meegeren admitted to having done not only the painting but also all the

Han van Meegeren grinding pigments

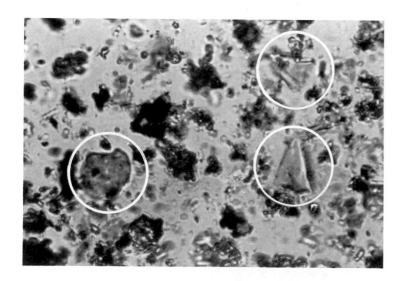

A telltale sign, diamond-shaped crystals of cobalt blue *(circled)* showed up in a microscopic examination of two of Van Meegeren's forgeries. Cobalt blue was a 19th Century discovery and of course had been unknown to Vermeer. Inadvertently Van Meegeren had bought a supply of what he thought was purest ultramarine blue, made from powdered lapis lazuli and the same as the blue used by Vermeer—but it had been doctored with the modern chemical.

A probing of the fakes revealed as many as five layers; an authentic old painting usually has only three—the varnish, the paint and the ground, applied directly to the canvas. Here a macrograph of a chipped-away portion of the *Last Supper* *(pages 180-181)* shows the first of two layers added by Van Meegeren to the existing three of the 17th Century painting he had used. This layer helped bring through to the new paint surface the network of cracks in the old painting underneath.

other "Vermeers" and two "De Hooghs" that had turned up during the War. The art world was incredulous, and an international commission was assembled to determine whether the disputed pictures were indeed fakes or originals. Some of the evidence assembled is displayed below, forming as intriguing a tale in its own right as that of the forger himself.

After being detained in prison for six weeks, Van Meegeren was placed in a house rented by the government, and there he began to paint, for the benefit of the authorities, his last "Vermeer," *Jesus amongst the Doctors.* He is shown at left, preparing pigments for this large painting, in the manner of 17th Century artists, by grinding them into a fine powder. Behind him is one of his own works, a portrait of a doctor that he had painted only two years before.

Courtroom spectator examining Van Meegeren's *Woman Taken in Adultery*

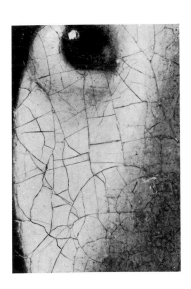
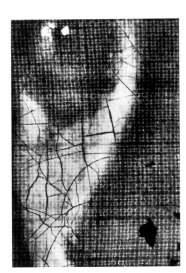
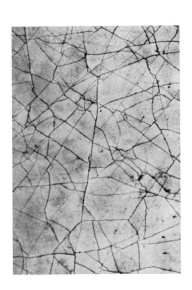
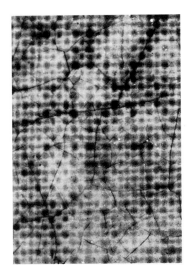

Two close-ups, the second a radiograph, show the network of cracks in a real Vermeer, *Girl in a Turban.* In both, the same cracks appear on and below the surface. When Van Meegeren's were subjected to a similar examination, the cracks failed to display the same kind of integrity *(photographs at right).* Only those coming through from the old paintings underneath could be detected at both levels. The others Van Meegeren had induced by rolling the finished paintings around a metal tube.

Induced cracks in Van Meegeren's *Christ and the Disciples at Emmaus* look like the real thing, but as the radiograph clearly shows, they fail to penetrate below the surface. Those cracks already existing in the old painting underneath, on the other hand, made their way up to the top. To make all the cracks look genuine, as though dust, dirt and grime had settled in them over the years, Van Meegeren carefully filled them in with black ink. In several forgeries the ink seeped beneath the paint and ran.

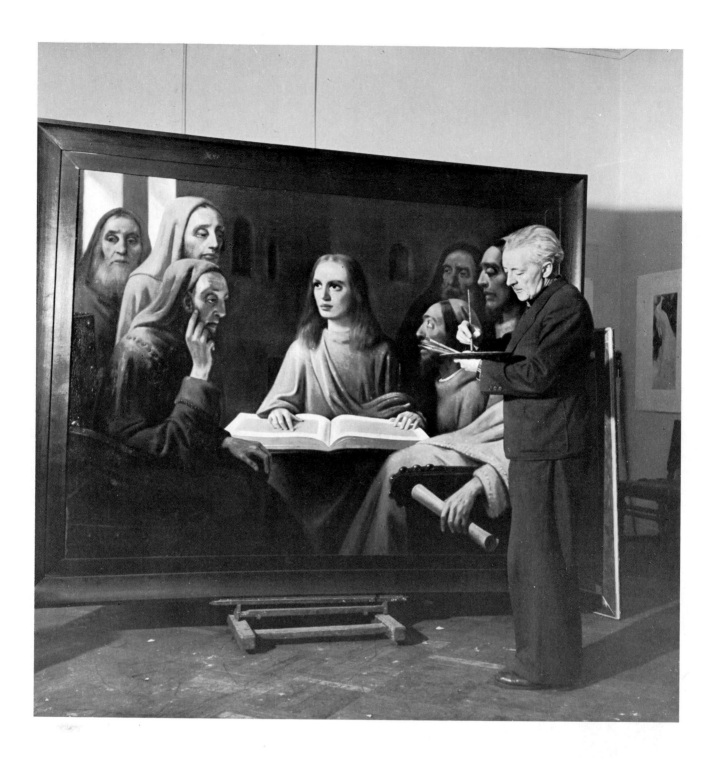

How could it all happen? This question was asked in the art world both before and after Van Meegeren's trial *(opposite)*. Admittedly, the first forgery had been successful and it was even considered a good painting; but the others were neither. Perhaps they were accepted because they appeared at the right time—during the War when real Vermeers were locked away, when people preferred to have tangible assets like paintings rather than cash and when the occupied Dutch were struggling to keep their treasures from falling into Nazi hands. Such was the secrecy surrounding each "discovery" that not until after the War did anyone realize how many new "Vermeers" —six in all—had turned up. Had this number been known, suspicions would certainly have been aroused earlier. As for Van Meegeren, his only reason for the forgeries was vindictiveness resulting from the failure of his career. Even near the end, as he painted a Vermeer-style canvas *(above)* at the request of authorities, he believed he would be acclaimed an equal of the great master. But he was convicted of fraud, sentenced to a year in prison, and died before he went to jail. What clings to his name is not the fame he sought, but simple notoriety.

Chronology: Artists of Vermeer's Era

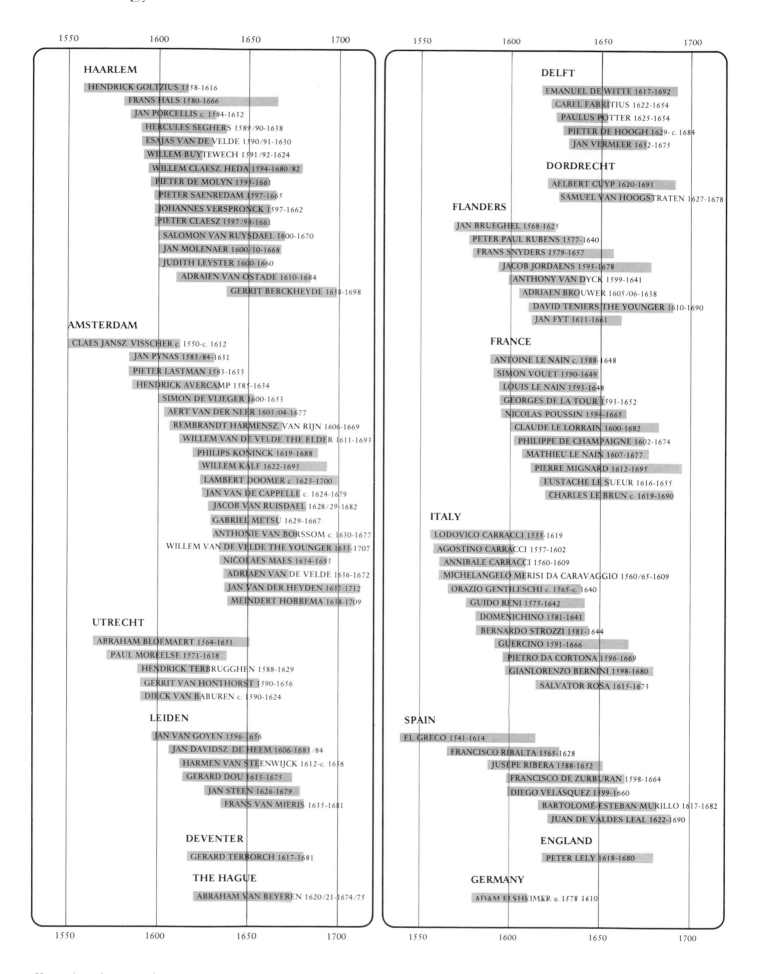

Vermeer's predecessors and contemporaries are grouped chronologically according to region or country. The bands correspond to the life-spans of the artists.

Bibliography   *Available in paperback.

CULTURAL AND HISTORICAL BACKGROUND

Blok, Petrus Johannes, *History of the People of the Netherlands,* Part III, G. P. Putnam's Sons, New York, 1900. A readable account of the wars with Spain.

Blunt, Wilfrid, *Tulipomania,* Penguin Books, London, 1950

Boxer, Charles R., *The Dutch Seaborne Empire, 1600-1800,* Alfred A. Knopf, New York, 1965. A political, social and commercial history of Holland. Reliable and informative.

*Friedrich, Carl J., *The Age of Baroque, 1610-1660,* Harper Torchbooks, 1962. A survey of Europe in the 17th Century.

Geyl, Pieter, *The Netherlands in the 17th Century,* New York, Barnes & Noble, 1961-1964, 3 vols. Reliable and complete.

*Hauser, Arnold, *The Social History of Art* (Vol. III), Vintage Books, New York, 1957. A historical view of the outburst of painting in 17th Century Holland.

Zumthor, Paul, *Daily Life in Rembrandt's Holland,* Macmillan Co., New York, 1963.

ART-HISTORICAL BACKGROUND

*Cogniat, Raymound, *Seventeenth Century Painting,* Compass Books, Viking Press, New York, 1964. A general survey.

*Friedländer, Max J., *Landscape, Portrait, Still-Life; Their Origin and Development,* Shocken Books, New York, 1963. Very important for general background in the varieties of Dutch painting.

Judson, J. Richard, *Gerrit van Honthorst,* Martinus Nijhoff, The Hague, 1959. An excellent monograph.

Knuttel, Gerard, *Adriaen Brouwer,* L.J.C. Boucher, The Hague, 1962. The most recent study of this popular artist.

Leymarie, Jean, *Dutch Painting,* translated by Stuart Gilbert, Editions d'Art, Albert Skira, Switzerland, 1956. A general informative survey.

Luttervelt, R. van, *Masterpieces from the Great Dutch Museums,* Harry N. Abrams, Inc., New York, 1961. A discriminating pictorial compilation.

Nicolson, Benedict, *Hendrick Terbrugghen,* Lund Humphries, London, 1958. A fine critique of an artist important for an understanding of Vermeer.

Rosenberg, J., S. Slive, E. H. Ter Kuile, *Dutch Art and Architecture, 1600-1800,* Penguin Books, London, 1966. The most recent authoritative survey.

Schendel, A.F.E. van, and B. Haak, *Art Treasures of the Rijksmuseum,* Harry N. Abrams, Inc., New York, 1966. Excellent reproductions.

Slatkes, Leonard J., *Dirck van Baburen,* Haentjens, Dekker & Gumbert, Utrecht, 1965. An illuminating monograph on a hitherto-neglected master of great interest in Vermeer studies.

Sterling, Charles, *Still Life Painting,* Universe Books, Inc., 1959. An important illustrated survey.

Swillens, P.T.A., Introduction to the Exhibition *Pieter Saenredam,* Central Museum, Utrecht, 1966. Presents a master with strong contemporary appeal.

Stechow, Wolfgang, *Dutch Landscape Painting of the Seventeenth Century,* Phaidon, London, 1966. A complete account of subject matter and style.

Wilenski, R. H., *Dutch Painting,* The Beechhurst Press, New York, 1955. Though slightly dated, a most provocative and readable work.

VERMEER, LIFE AND WORK

Bloch, Vitale, *All the Paintings of Vermeer,* Hawthorn Books, Inc., New York, 1963.

De Vries, A. B., *In the Light of Vermeer,* Five Centuries of Painting. Catalogue for an exhibition at The Hague, June-Sept. 1966.

De Vries, A. B., *Vermeer,* B. T. Batsford Ltd., London, 1948. Though dated, still useful.

Goldscheider, Ludwig, *Jan Vermeer,* Phaidon Publishers, Inc., New York, 1958. A clear and able study.

Gowing, Lawrence, *Vermeer,* Faber and Faber, London, 1952. A fine interpretation of the artist, with unique critical insights.

Mayor, A. Hyatt, "The Photographic Eye," Bulletin of the Metropolitan Museum of Art, November, 1937. An important contribution to the camera obscura hypothesis.

Seymour, Charles Jr., "Dark Chamber and Light-Filled Room: Vermeer and the Camera Obscura," The Art Bulletin, Vol. XLVI, No. 3, Sept. 1964. The first presentation of evidence linking the camera obscura hypothesis with specific paintings.

Schwarz, Heinrich, "Vermeer and the Camera Obscura," Pantheon, Vol. XXIV, No. 3, May June, 1966.

Swillens, P.T.A., *Johannes Vermeer,* Spectrum Publishers, Utrecht, 1950. A historian's unusually careful and illuminating compilation of the facts of Vermeer's life and career.

THE VAN MEEGEREN FORGERIES

Coremans, Dr. P. B., *Van Meegeren's Faked Vermeers and De Hooghs,* translated by A. Hardy and C. M. Hutt, Cassell & Co., Ltd., London, 1949. The authoritative scientific investigation of the forgeries by the most respected expert on this subject.

Godley, John, *The Master Forger,* Wilfred Funk, Inc., 1950. A biography commissioned by Van Meegeren's family.

Moiseiwitsch, Maurice, *The Van Meegeren Mystery,* Arthur Baker, Ltd., 1964. A general account, accenting the sensational aspects of the case.

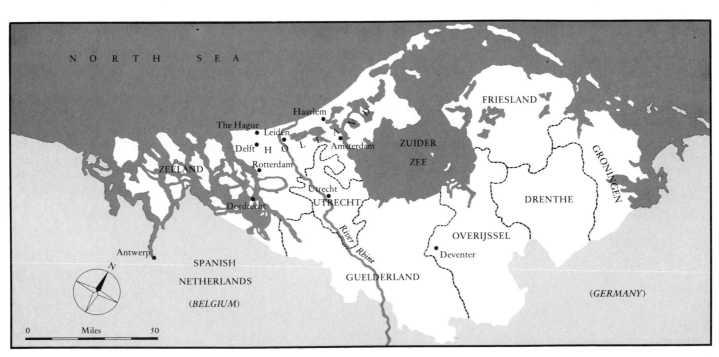

A Map of the United Provinces in Vermeer's Time

Acknowledgments

The editors of this book wish to thank the following: Robert G. Barclay, Second Vice President, Chase Manhattan Bank; Sir Alfred Beit, Blessington, Ireland; Mrs. Thomas N. Bently, Acting Registrar, Toledo Museum of Art; P. de Boer, Amsterdam; Anselmo Carini, Publications, Art Institute of Chicago; Mrs. Ruth Dundas, Chief, Publications Service, and Michael Mahoney, Museum Curator, National Gallery of Art, Washington, D.C.; Ellen Franklin, Publicity Assistant, and Claus Virch, Associate Curator of Paintings, The Metropolitan Museum of Art, New York; Mr. Th. Hoog, Haarlem, The Netherlands; B. de Geus van den Heuvel, Loenen aan de Vecht, The Netherlands; Mrs. Hans Hofmann, New York; Marian Willard Johnson and Lucy Mitton, Willard Gallery, New York; Samuel M. Kootz, New York; Mme. J. van Meegeren-Oerlemans, Laren, The Netherlands; Menzo de Munck, Zwolle, The Netherlands; Claes A. Philip, Stockholm; W. Reineke, Amersfoort, The Netherlands; Dr. and Mrs. Allan Roos, San Francisco; Raymond de Roover, Professor of History, Brooklyn College, New York; René Sneyers, Acting Director, Central Laboratories of Belgian Museums; Wolfgang Stechow, Lecturer in Art, Oberlin College, Oberlin, Ohio; Diggory Venn, Administrative Assistant, Museum of Fine Arts, Boston; J. Howard Whittemore, Naugatuck, Connecticut; Mr. and Mrs. Charles B. Wrightsman, New York.

Picture Credits

SLIPCASE:
Erich Lessing from Magnum

END PAPERS:
Front: © Rijksmuseum, Amsterdam
Back: Handzeichnungen Meister aus der Sammlung Dr. C. Hofstede de Groot im Haag, B. Tauchnitz, Leipzig, 1923, plate 14, courtesy New York Public Library.

CHAPTER 1: 8—Metropolitan Museum of Art photo. 12—Reproduced from *A Short History of Science and Scientific Thought* by F. Sherwood Taylor. © 1949, by W. W. Norton Company, Inc., New York. 15—By permission of the British Museum, London. 17—Frank Lerner. 18—Paulus Leeser. 19—Herbert Orth. 20, 21—Metropolitan Museum of Art photo. 22—Derek Bayes. 23—Harry Baskerville. 24—Yves Debraine; Frank Lerner. 25—Frank Lerner—Art Institute of Chicago photo. 26—Eddy Van der Veen. 27—Frank Lerner.

CHAPTER 2: 28—Hein de Bouter. 34, 35—© Rijksmuseum, Amsterdam. 41—© Rijksmuseum, Amsterdam. 42, 43—© Rijksmuseum, Amsterdam; Municipal Archives, Haarlem, photo. 44, 45—© Rijksmuseum, Amsterdam. 46, 47—By courtesy of the Trustees of the British Museum, London. 48, 49—Hein de Bouter. 52—© Rijksmuseum, Amsterdam. 53—Lee Boltin. 54, 55—Eric Schaal.

CHAPTER 3: 56—Eric Schaal. 59—Koninklijke Bibliotheek photo. 61—Municipality of Delft. 65—Eddy Van der Veen. 66—Pierre Boulat—Eric Schaal. 67—Robert S. Crandall—Hans Hammarskiold / TIO. 68—Boymans van Beuningen Museum, Rotterdam, photo. 69—Boymans van Beuningen Museum, Rotterdam, photo—Eric Schaal. 70—Eric Schaal. 71—Eddy Van der Veen.

CHAPTER 4: 72—Metropolitan Museum of Art photo. 74—Eric Schaal—Frans Hals Museum, Haarlem, photo by A. Dingjan. 77—John R. Freeman. 78—Metropolitan Museum of Art photo. 80, 81—Eric Schaal. 82, 83—Eric Schaal; Toledo Museum of Art photo. 84, 85—Eric Schaal. 86, 87—Eddy Van der Veen. 88—Eric Schaal. 89—Eric Schaal—© Rijksmuseum, Amsterdam. 90, 91—Hein de Bouter. 92—Metropolitan Museum of Art photo—Bayerische Staatsgemäldesammlungen, Munich, photo. 93—Hein de Bouter.

CHAPTER 5: 94—National Gallery, London photo. 98—© Rijksmuseum, Amsterdam. 101—© Rijksmuseum, Amsterdam. 104, 105—Metropolitan Museum of Art photo. 106—© University of Oxford, Ashmolean Museum. 107—Statens Museum for Kunst, Copenhagen, photo. 108, 109—Metropolitan Museum of Art photo—© Teyler's Museum, Haarlem; Staatliche Museen, Berlin, photo by Walter Steinkopf. 110, 111—Boymans van Beuningen Museum, Rotterdam, photo; Pierre Belzeaux from Rapho Guillumette. 112, 113—© Rijksmuseum, Amsterdam. 114, 115—Hein de Bouter. 116, 117—Left: Art Institute of Chicago photo—Eric Schaal. Right: Derek Bayes. 118, 119—Eric Schaal; © Rijksmuseum, Amsterdam.

CHAPTER 6: 120—Eric Schaal. 122—Delft Municipal Archives. 129—Eddy Van der Veen. 130—Derek Bayes. 131, 132, 133—Eric Schaal. 134—Reproduced by Gracious Permission of Her Majesty the Queen, © reserved. 135—Stadelsches Kunstinstitut, Frankfurt, photo. 136—Frick Collection photo. 137—Frank Lerner. 138, 139—Gernsheim Collection, University of Texas, Austin, photo; Reproduced from *Apiaria Universae Philosophiae Mathematicae* Bononia, 1642, Apiar VI, Progim III, p. 43, courtesy Charles Seymour Jr.; Reproduced from Kircher, *Ars Magna Lucis et Umbrae*, 1646 ed., courtesy Charles Seymour Jr.; Reproduced from Zahn, *Oculus Artificialis*, 1701 ed., courtesy Charles Seymour Jr.—drawings by Lowell Hess. 140—Eric Schaal. 141—Eric Schaal—National Gallery of Art, Washington, photo by Henry Beville. Left: Yale Art Gallery photo by Emidio De Cusati, courtesy Charles Seymour Jr. Center and right: National Gallery of Art, Washington, photos by Henry Beville, courtesy Charles Seymour Jr. 142, 143—Left: Yale Art Gallery photo by Emidio De Cusati, courtesy Charles Seymour Jr. Center and right: National Gallery of Art, Washington, photos by Henry Beville, courtesy Charles Seymour Jr.

CHAPTER 7: 144—Eddy Van der Veen. 147—Stadelsches Kunstinstitut, Frankfurt, photo—(2) After P.T.A. Swillens in *Johannes Vermeer*, Publishers Het Spectrum, Utrecht, 1950, plate 53b. 150—Reproduced from André Blum, *Vermeer et Thoré-Bürger*, Editions du Mont-Blanc, Genève, 1946. 153—National Gallery of Art, Washington, photo. 154, 155—Lee Boltin; National Gallery of Art, Washington, photo. 156—Isabella Stewart Gardner Museum photo by Henry Beville. 157—Frick Collection photo—National Gallery, London, photo. 158 through 161—Eric Schaal. 162, 163—Frank Lerner.

CHAPTER 8: 164 through 167—Erich Lessing from Magnum. 168—Tom Scott. 175—George Rodger from Magnum. 176, 177—© A.C.L., Brussels. 178—Anefo D. Raucamp from Pix Inc. 179—Top: Alinari. Bottom: © A.C.L., Brussels. 180, 181—© A.C.L., Brussels except lower right: © A.C.L., Brussels courtesy Douwes Brothers. 182, 183—Top: George Rodger from Magnum. Bottom: © A.C.L., Brussels. 184—George Rodger from Magnum. 185—Yale Joel. 186—Chart by George V. Kelvin. 187—Map by Rafael D. Palacios.

188

Index

Numerals in italics indicate a picture of the subject mentioned. Unless otherwise identified, all listed art works are by Vermeer. Dimensions are given in inches; height precedes width.

The typeface employed in this book is called Janson, after Anton Janson, the Dutch typefounder who popularized it in Leipzig in the late 17th Century. The face was first cut, however, by Nicholas Kis, a Hungarian working in Amsterdam in the 1680s.